Comes
THE
Dark

P.A. TURNER

Text copyright © 2018 P.A. Turner
All rights reserved.

First Print Edition 2018 Dark Ink Press

www.darkink-press.com

ISBN-13 978-0-9997016-9-0
ISBN 0-9997016-9-X

Cover design by Michelle Arzu

Printed in the United States of America

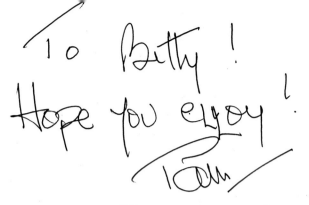

To Bithy !
Hope you enjoy !
Paul

Comes the Dark

P.A.Turner

Paul T

To all victims and survivors of
sexual exploitation:
Believe in yourselves.

There is help out there.
Never give up.

FOREWORD

Helping a childless woman adopt; finding a happy, safe, foster home for a neglected child, supporting a long-term addict to get his life back on course, building a trusting, working relationship with someone suffering a severe mental illness, or someone with learning difficulties, are some of my satisfying memories as a social worker.

Then, there are the downright odd memories. Jimmy answering the door of his multi-story flat dressed only in a kilt and war-paint, while brandishing a snooker-cue. This almost caused my eight-month pregnant colleague to give birth on the spot. And, of course there are the scary ones. The distraught mother whose three children had just been removed into care, holding a knife to the throat of her youngest.

Or, those which reached so far within me that they affected the rest of my life.

It all began one rainy, Friday afternoon when I was on Intake duty, which means I had to see anyone who walked into the office and try to help them *'fix'* their problems. I'm embarrassed to admit that I was clock-watching and somewhat fed-up with the repetitive stream of young mothers who regularly appeared before the weekend, complaining about lost purses and non-payment of benefits. At this time, social work had a legal duty to help if they had no money to feed their children and 'help' usually meant money. Nowadays, if they are lucky, they will be given vouchers for foodbanks. Ten minutes before closing time, I checked the waiting room. One person remained, scruffy and hunched in the corner.

Finn was seventeen and homeless, frozen and soaked to the skin. He was small for his age, frightened and starving. We made him mugs of tea and soup, and my colleague ran over to the local shop to buy sandwiches and crisps, which he wolfed like there was no tomorrow. By dint of much persuasion at that time on a Friday, we managed to get him into a hostel where at least he would be warm, dry and fed. His mixture of gratitude and suspicion lasted the whole of the next few weeks, until he began to trust and told me his story.

At the age of four, Finn's mother abandoned him in McDonald's, saying she was just nipping out for cigarettes. Convinced she would one day find him, he survived a series of foster homes, until at the age of ten, reality set in. He gave up waiting and began to act out his grief and anger. By the time he was eleven, skipping school and being generally antisocial, he was pronounced 'out-with-control,' and admitted to a residential school.

The school, like others at that time, was run along military lines, with a chain of command beginning with 'The Colonel", who could do no wrong, and older boys as corporals, who kept discipline. Finn never understood why he had to polish the soles of his boots every day. For the next four years Finn was subjected to physical and sexual assaults, by the Colonel and others like him. At first, he tried to tell and to fight, which earned him beatings, until he had to give up and accept the only way to survive was to obey the rules until he could escape. At the age of sixteen, a Scottish Childrens' Hearing freed him from the care system, only for him to fall into the hands of street-based predators. After months of prostitution, shop-lifting and drug-taking, he fled to another city, eventually turning up on our doorstep.

I worked with Finn for the next year until he died of a drug overdose. But the memory of him and other survivors of abuse and sexual exploitation permeated my personal and professional attitudes and values from then on. There were many times throughout my career that I struggled with the disbelief of others, including colleagues. Even today, despite media exposure of monsters like Cyril Smith and Jimmy Saville, there are people who, for whatever reason, simply cannot accept that paedophiles exist and that worldwide human slavery remains as prevalent today as in Viking times.

It was never my intention to set myself up as any kind of "expert" in this area, in which there are many books on the subject, but I wanted to perhaps raise my own little bit of awareness, and in doing so, honour the memory of Finn and others like him. So, I decided to write a novel, with characters whose story demonstrates that with help, people can recover and live normal lives - and dedicate it to the strength and resilience of those survivors.

Thank you for buying this book, which I hope you will accept in the spirit in which it was written. I apologise for any inaccuracies, which are entirely my own.

P.A. Turner

"Any child may be deemed to have been sexually abused when any person(s), by design or neglect, exploits the child, directly or indirectly in any activity intended to lead to the sexual arousal or other forms of gratification of that person or any other person(s), including organised networks. This definition holds whether or not there has been genital contact and whether or not the child is said to have initiated or consented to the behaviour."
(Scottish Office)

PART ONE

Chapter One

It was the day of Kyle's release and he could hardly contain his excitement. A glance at the calendar to make sure and, there it was ringed in red. He raised his hand to fist pump the air and froze. The heavy footsteps in the corridor passed his door. He sighed, his good mood dissipating as he gazed around the dismal room he'd slept in for the last four years.

The two beds with their faded football team duvets and matching green and white lamp shades. The ash-smeared bible, from which they were supposed to read every night, propping up the tin ashtray. His turn to empty it, but he'd leave it to Nathan as a parting gift. Not out the window, since the night the whole lot landed on the janitor's head; the man's screams of outrage drowning their muffled giggles. He heard more footsteps, boys' voices as they went to their rooms to change for P.E. An image filled his mind of the P.E. teacher leering at them in the showers. His relief at never having to go through that again was overtaken by one of the bursts of rage he had difficulty controlling. He jumped as the bedroom door burst open.

Nathan hurtled through. "Hi, Kyle." Nathan did a double take. "Wow, what's going on?" Unzipping as he went, he galloped to the toilet.

Kyle had to raise his voice to be heard over the loud peeing sound. "My last Panel, remember? It's my sixteenth birthday."

The toilet flushed, and Nathan came through, zipping himself up. "Oh, yeah, forgot. Happy birthday and all that. Me next year." He stood at the sink to wash his hands and glanced at Kyle in the mirror. "Haircut too? How'd you get him to cut it so short?" He tightened his blond ponytail.

Kyle shrugged, and smoothed back his dark copper hair in the mirror. "Just asked him. Told him it was my last Panel and . . . freedom!" he yelled in imitation of Mel Gibson.

Nathan grinned and slapped him on the shoulder. "So, this is goodbye." He laughed, voice fading, as they stared at one another's reflections.

Kyle's throat tightened. He almost reached for a hug.

"Can I have your iPod?"

"Piss off." Kyle laughed in relief. "I won that fair and square and it's in my pocket." In the mirror, he slid his tie beneath his collar. "And don't boss the new guy around too much."

Nathan snorted. "No chance. Have you seen the size of him? "Least I won't have to put up with your farting any longer." He stuck two fingers in the air as he left.

Kyle swallowed his sadness, and fumbled with his tie again. It was squint and the knot was too big. He tugged it straight, squashed it between his fingers and pulled down his shirt cuffs to hide his scars. Another glance to smooth his hair. Nice length, not scalped, but not girly either. "Good afternoon." He smiled at his reflection, then closed his mouth because he looked like a shark. "Hello," he mumbled, looked himself in the eye, and recognised the fear and sadness reflected in his grey gaze.

He heard a knock on the door.

"You 'bout ready, Kyle?"

A deep breath and a glance in the mirror to check his eyes gave nothing away. "Yeah, almost, Steve. Come in."

The tall, well-built man, who could pick up a boy under each arm, grinned as he held the door wide. "Fancy a McDonald's, seeing it's your birthday?"

<>

Stuffed from his burger, fries, ice-cream and two cokes, Kyle was surprised when Steve parked near a building he'd never been to before and led him up a carpeted staircase. He had always been rehearsed at what to say at Hearings, but this time, Steve hadn't said a word. His confusion grew when he saw Spike waiting at the top.

"You're late," Spike said, grasping his arm.

Kyle was conscious of a fluttery, empty feeling in his stomach. Why was he being escorted to the Hearing, when he couldn't wait to get there, he wondered.

Spike halted before a polished door marked 'Private', knocked and waited. At the sound of a voice from within, he opened it and nudged Kyle forward.

Kyle stumbled to a halt, unable to breathe. It wasn't a Children's Hearing. No table with three Panel members awaited him. There was only Bill, the man who had stolen his childhood.

"Come and sit down, boy." Bill waved him to a chair before his ornate desk. "We need to have a chat."

"Move," Spike growled, pushing him forward and into the chair.

Transfixed, Kyle stared at Bill's fat, ugly face.

"Now, that's better, isn't it?" Bill smiled. "Do you want a coke? Get the boy a coke, Steve."

Kyle jerked as the cold can landed on his lap.

"Go on, then, you enjoy. I know what boys like."

As Kyle fumbled with the can, Bill suddenly left his chair and moving fast for such a big man, plucked it from his numb fingers, popped it open and handed it back. The stink of old cigarettes was overpowering.

"Drink up."

Kyle drank and swallowed a burp.

Wary, he watched as Bill folded his arms and leaned back against the desk. "Well now, this is a big day for you." He paused and asked in a peremptory tone, "Isn't it?"

Kyle looked down at the can. "Yes, sir."

"Look at me, boy."

Quaking inside, Kyle raised his head.

Bill was smiling, head tilted. "Aww, such pretty eyes. And a new suit and haircut, if I'm not mistaken?" He smiled approval at Steve.

Kyle forced a nod as he strangled the coke can.

"Yes, we look after our boys."

Kyle flinched as Bill leaned forward. He touched Kyle's throat, adjusted his tie and stood up again.

"You certainly look the part of a young man setting out on life's new adventures," Bill said, his Glaswegian accent sounding stronger.

As the hard, shiny eyes studied him, Kyle began to tremble.

Bill's mouth stretched in an unpleasant smile. "What do you want to do with your life, boy?" he suddenly asked.

"I . . . I don't know, sir."

Bill frowned.

"Maybe, maybe work in a bank, sir," Kyle said in desperation.

"He's good at maths, boss," Steve commented.

Bill's eyebrows rose. "Is he now? And English? What about English?"

"He has six GCEs." Steve sounded proud.

"A clever boy, then." Bill smiled, showing shining white teeth, which Kyle knew were at odds with his stinking breath. "I had no idea I'd been shagging such a clever boy."

The other men laughed.

Kyle looked down at the floor.

"Look at me, boy. Show that pretty face."

Stomach churning, Kyle stared into those speculative eyes.

"I don't think you have the experience for a bank," Bill said, "What do you think, Spike?"

"I think the Panel will make him stay on at school, Bill."

Kyle couldn't breathe. Icy prickles ran down his spine.

"He's right." Bill sighed in a resigned way. "They can do that, if they don't think you're ready for the outside world. Spike should know. It happened to him. You don't want it happening to you, do you son?"

Kyle had to work saliva into his mouth before he could speak. "N . . . no, sir." It came out as a squeak.

With a satisfied nod, Bill relaxed against the desk. "So, what we'll do is organise a care-plan. Steve will tell the Panel that you can do work experience with me for the next two years. Filing, general office work, that sort of thing and your social worker will agree." He paused. "Who's the social worker?" he asked Steve.

"Karen Bullock. She'll do what she's told."

Bill nodded and turned back to Kyle. "Now, now, there's no need for that. Bill will look after you."

Nauseated, Kyle suffered the fat fingers stroking his tears. "You're such a handsome lad. I don't think I've given you enough attention lately." Bill mused, his smelly forefinger tracing Kyle's mouth, pushing between his lips, making him want to retch. "Okay, almost time for your Panel." The finger withdrew.

Kyle half turned to leave.

"Haven't you forgotten to thank me?"

He faltered and turned back.

Bill unzipped.

Chapter Two

Two Years Later

With a sigh, Kyle helped himself to a slice of pizza. It had been a long day, and he felt tired. Due to being promoted, he now had access to Bill's inner circle and more importantly, his database. He took meeting minutes and typed reports about trafficking children from one city to another, about safe houses and costs involved. He tried to pretend it was all about tins of beans and packets of cheese and not think about the blowjobs he had to give to seal deals for Bill. Sometimes, Bill gave him presents of chocolates and, once, a watch which had someone's initials on the back. Sometimes, if he was particularly pleased about a deal he'd struck, he gave Kyle cash and told him to buy clothes. Although never alone, it was a brief escape.

As the months dragged on, his thinking had changed, and sometimes, he was almost overwhelmed by the horror and collusion he was trapped in. He knew he had to get out before he went mad, or worse, didn't care anymore. On impulse one day, he'd begun copying important data on to a pen drive and hiding it in his sock. At night, he pushed it into a hole in his mattress and by day, a tear he'd made in the lining of his jackets. Although he knew they'd kill him if they found out, he felt better knowing it was there.

"What's happening tonight, then?" asked Terry, bringing Kyle back to the present. All he really wanted was to have a shower and climb into bed, but this ritual of sharing a meal and chatting was an important part of surviving in the flat.

"Dunno, he hasn't phoned yet." Kyle shrugged. The parties didn't concern him. He had a job.

"Plenty time yet. It's only six. Hope I'm not needed." Sean winked at Kyle. "Could hardly sit down for a week last time. Good tips, though."

Kyle smiled back. He liked Sean. His camp behaviour and casual acceptance of the situation irritated him sometimes, but his kindness made up for it. The other two at the table were talking about football, which he hated. Terry, the good-looking blond one whom Kyle thought looked like a popstar, was older than the rest of them. He took a leadership role at times, keeping Jason in check. At seventeen, Jason was the youngest. He seemed to want to fight all the time, and Kyle avoided him as much as possible.

"It's fucking true, man." Jason insisted. "There were five in front of the goals."

"Huh, Beckham." Sean snorted, flinching when Jason rounded on him, face red.

"What the fuck would you know? You only play girl's games."

"No, I don't."

"Cool it, both of you," Terry said. "It doesn't matter how many were guarding the goal Jaz, you still scored. Well done."

The way Jason smiled happily, anger forgotten, made Kyle wonder, not for the first time, about his maturity level. There had been boys in the school with learning difficulties, and sometimes Jason reminded him of them. Sean too seemed younger than his eighteen years as he stuck his tongue out at Jason.

"Right, we're on dishes, Jaz," Terry announced. "You two clear the table. If he doesn't phone, you can watch Corrie."

Kyle disposed of the pizza boxes in the bin, while Sean brought a cloth to wipe the table.

"Are you watching telly tonight?" Sean asked. "That new sci-fi starts at nine."

Kyle shook his head. "No, I'm knackered. Having an early night, sorry." He knew how Sean liked to cuddle in beside him on the couch. Sean's face fell, but before more was said, the front door slammed, and they all stopped what they were doing and stared at each other.

The kitchen door opened, and Spike surveyed the room; cold gaze resting on them, one by one, his spiky, bleached blond hair trembling in the harsh ceiling light.

As he warily watched Bill's right-hand man, Kyle noticed that he had a rip in the left arm of his long, leather coat. The one he was so proud of; bought on e-Bay for $5000 and, he claimed, had belonged to his T.V. vampire hero.

"Hi, boys," Spike finally said, and they all murmured in response. "Big night tonight."

"Who's going, Spike?" Terry asked.

"Get me a coffee, Sean," Spike said, striding into the living room.

"It . . . it's just that I was hoping for the night off," Terry continued. "Hardly seen my girlfriend in ages."

"She'll just have to do without your cock tonight. It's needed elsewhere," Spike said, sitting in an armchair beside the gas fire, legs spread wide.

Sean placed a coffee mug on the hearth and hurried back to the others.

"You have one hour to get ready, showered, shaved, nails done and dressed." Without another glance, Spike pulled out his mobile and began texting.

As Kyle turned to leave with the others, the voice stopped him.

"You too, Kyle."

"Me?" Surprised, Kyle turned back. "But I've been working all day."

"So? You can work all night too," Spike snapped. "It's all-hands-on-deck. Get a move on and tell Sean to put some eyeliner on you."

Dressed in fresh clothes, Kyle tried hard not to blink as Sean held down his lower eyelid and scraped away with a black pencil.

"Stand still and stop fidgeting. If I poke you in the eye, you'll know all about it. There now, what d'you think?" Sean held up a mirror.

The black outline seemed to make his eyes pop out of his face. Kyle wanted to scrub it off.

"D'you want some lipstick too?" Sean asked.

"No way."

"Suits you," Sean commented, gazing at him. "You have lovely eyes and your long lashes are to die for."

"Right!" Spike yelled from the next room. "Five minutes and we're leaving."

They trooped into the living room to be inspected.

"You need a haircut, Terry."

"Yes, Spike."

"And when I said nails done, Sean, I didn't mean glitter nail varnish."

With a chuckle, Spike lightly cuffed Sean's head. "Maybe we should put you in a dress tonight."

Chapter Three

When the black mini-bus drew up before the mansion blazing with lights, Kyle climbed out and glanced around the car-park. Several uniformed drivers hung around big, shiny cars, chatting and smoking. From the open front door, someone called his name, and for an instant, he considered bolting, then unwillingly dragging his feet, he obeyed.

Before he entered the room, he could hear their voices.

"I'm a slutty rent boy." Jason laughed.

"Yeah, we know," Terry replied.

"Look at these jeans," Jason said as Kyle walked in. "More holes than jeans. My arse is falling out."

It was like the gym dressing-room at school. A bench against each wall, with a row of hooks above, most hung with clothing, some covered in plastic.

"Wow! I'm a fairy!" Sean said in delight as he shook out a glittery pink dress.

"You can say that again." Jason giggled, then his face changed as he saw Kyle. "You've to find the outfit with your name on and get changed."

"Yes, I know," Kyle muttered. As he walked around checking coat hangers, he remembered the first time he'd had to attend one of Bill's parties. Twelve years old and small for his age, he'd been terrified when they dressed him in a school uniform and pushed him into the centre of a circle of waiting men.

He ripped open the plastic covering his new outfit and groaned. The harness was soft, black leather with a silver medallion in the centre. There was a matching spiked dog collar with a lead attached. A name tag on the collar read SUB. He sighed at the inevitability of it all. "Fuck's sake," he swore.

Half dressed, the three others joined him.

"So, what's the problem?" Terry asked, poking around the plastic. "It looks like a gladiator costume."

"Why give *him* that?" Jason was angry, his colour high. "A skinny, wee arse like him."

"You're just jealous," Sean said.

Jason turned on him. "No, I'm not."

Sean pushed his wavy, blond hair behind his ear with delicate fingers. "Cool it, Jaz. It doesn't matter."

"I'm not fucking jealous." Jason's voice rose, and Sean took a step back.

Kyle tensed, preparing for the usual upsurge of aggression.

"Hey, Jaz. C'mere and look at this," Terry exclaimed, distracting him. Between finger and thumb, he held a thin, leather belt with a dangling mesh pouch.

"Too wee for me." He laughed, swinging it back and forward.

"And me." Jason grabbed it. "What about you, creep? Show us what you've got." He began a chorus of 'show us your cock,' in a singsong voice.

When Terry laughingly joined in, Kyle sighed.

"Piss off," he said, tired of the banter.

"Leave him alone," Sean yelled.

"What the hell is going on here?" Spike walked into the room, scattering them with a glare. "You should be ready. Bill's waiting." He focussed on Kyle. "You haven't even started yet. Get a move on."

Kyle stood inside the doorway as Jason swaggered past, head thrown back, thumbs hooked in his belt. He did a round of the room, stopping every so often to thrust his pelvis at the noisy, ogling audience.

As usual, the presence of women at these auctions always made the situation seedier and more humiliating for Kyle. He felt sweat trickle down his chest and back as Terry, in leather motorcycle gear, pushed him out of the way and stomped into the room.

"Get ready," Spike whispered in his ear. He yanked Sean closer. "Run around and tow him behind you like he doesn't want to go."

"He doesn't." Sean grinned.

Spike handed him the end of the lead. "The more he fights, the higher the price. Hold back, Kyle. Pretend you're a reluctant sub."

Before Kyle could react, Sean took off at a run, forcing him to stumble after. The collar dug into his neck, and the wall of sound which greeted their appearance shocked him. As he grabbed at the collar to ease the pressure Sean jerked hard on the lead, and he fell to his hands and knees. He could hear laughter, and voices calling out numbers and looked up to see Sean wagging a chiding finger at him.

"Two thousand," a voice called over the hubbub. "Each."

"Shit," Sean whispered as the room quietened. "She's a bastard."

As he rose to his feet, Kyle followed his gaze to a striking-looking woman with long, black hair, leather-clad legs crossed, seated in an armchair next to Bill.

With a beaming smile, Bill beckoned them over and pointed to the floor in front of the chairs.

"The fairy is Sean, and the young Sub is Kyle," Bill announced. "Boys, this is Cathy, a good friend of mine. I expect you to make her very happy."

As soon as he sat down, Kyle was yanked back by the hair and he stared up into the heavily made-up face. As he had often noticed before with such people, the eyes seemed lifeless. The second thing he noticed was the prominent Adam's Apple.

"Kyle, is it?" Cathy asked, studying him. "Is that his real name?"

"Mmm, yes."

"*Is* he a Sub?" She tugged on Kyle's hair, making him grimace in pain.

"He's whatever you want him to be."

"His eyes are quite stunning."

"He's cute and experienced." Bill smiled at Kyle. "Small for his age too. Good for business."

"He'll do." She nodded, releasing Kyle and turning her attention to Sean, who was playing with the folds of his glittery skirt. "And what about you, my sweet? Have we met before?"

"Yes, ma'am." Sean simpered. "At Halloween. I was an elf."

Embarrassed by Sean's behaviour, Kyle turned away and glanced around. Jason, Terry and some other boys were on their knees busy with clients, and after all the years, he still felt nauseated at the thought of what was to come.

He paused. There was something familiar about the back of a blond head. He stared for a moment, then the man the boy was servicing groaned and pushed him off. Kyle's stomach flipped. He should have known Nathan's fate would be the same as his own, but seeing him here, like this, stunned him. The intervening two years melted away, and he was standing in the grotty bedroom they had shared.

"New clothes. What's going on?" Nathan asked as he hurtled past to the toilet.

"My last Children's Hearing." Kyle raised his voice over the loud peeing sound. "I'm sixteen today."

17

The toilet flushed and Nathan appeared zipping himself up. "Yeah, forgot. Happy birthday and all that. Me, next year."

A jerk on the collar brought him back to reality.

"Up, the pair of you," Cathy said. "I didn't spend good money to watch other people getting off." She flung the lead at him and headed for the door.

As he followed her tall figure, Kyle was conscious of someone falling into step beside him. He looked around and found himself gazing into Nathan's blue eyes.

"You're looking good, Kyle."

Nathan's familiar smile almost broke his heart. "Are you okay?" he asked.

They'd reached the hall, with an intersection to the front door, another corridor to the right and the staircase.

Nathan winked. "I'm going this way," he said indicating the stairs.

As one, they reached a hand towards each other, but before their fingers could touch, Spike's voice cracked into the silence.

"Aww, how sweet. Get a move on, both of you." He pushed Nathan one way and yanked Kyle towards the front door. "We'll pick you up in the morning. Sean's got your clothes."

Chapter Four

As soon as they were in the rear seat, Kyle scrabbled inside his bag. All his clothing seemed to be there. On the pretence that he was cold, he retrieved his jacket and pulled it on, stuffing his hands in the pockets. The car began to move as he nervously poked his finger through the hole in the right pocket and into the lining.

"Have you boys eaten?" Cathy asked from the front passenger seat.

"Yes, thank you," Sean replied.

Kyle sighed in relief when he touched the smooth oblong. As he watched the dark countryside roll by, he gently rubbed the pen drive between finger and thumb, and hoped it would bring him luck in the night ahead. Sean shuffled closer until he was leaning against him and laid his head on Kyle's shoulder. He was trembling, and automatically, Kyle put his arm around him.

Cathy fiddled with the dashboard, and the car began to heat up.

As Sean began to softly snore, Kyle leaned against the door and stared out into the night. Every so often, as they passed through villages, lights broke the darkness and once when the car stopped at a junction he had the wild impulse to jump out. He reached for the door handle, but Sean's body against his own stopped him. He couldn't leave him behind to face the consequences. As they sped on, he caught a glimpse of a signpost which said that Glasgow was twenty miles further on. It was where Bill's offices were, and he knew he could find his way around, but they turned the other way and plunged along more tree-lined roads, confusing him as they twisted and turned.

Finally, they stopped at a set of gates, which the driver opened by remote control, and on through a well-lit, tree-lined avenue. They pulled up at a big, modern house which seemed all glass and he shook Sean awake. The interior light came on as Cathy climbed out. Kyle pulled the door handle, but nothing happened. He pushed his shoulder against it. The driver turned and with a wolfish grin, flicked a switch on the dash, and the door opened.

"I'll see you in the morning, Brian," Cathy said, heading for the front door. "Come boys." She led them to a glass lift and waved them inside. "Go up to the third-floor bathroom and use the facilities. I want you naked and spotless, inside and out." She slammed the door, and the lift began to rise.

They looked at one another in the dim interior. "Have you had her before?" Kyle asked. Sean nodded. "Did she hurt you a lot?"

Sean shrugged. "She's a Dom, and she's rough. At Halloween, I could hardly walk. She likes to use the whip."

Kyle had a memory of Sean's swollen face and bleeding body. "Was that her? They're not supposed to hurt us as much as that," he hissed. "What did Spike say?"

"You heard Bill. Cathy's his pal."

"Well, she's not doing that again," Kyle vowed.

The leather-covered door studded with brass squares stood half open.

"This is her play-room," Sean said, pushing it wider.

Kyle looked around in trepidation. He had been in similar rooms before, although this one was like a gym, with barbells on the floor and fitness equipment. His gaze came to rest on the black St. Andrew's cross attached to one wall, and he shuddered at the thought of hanging there at anyone's mercy.

"I don't think you're quite ready for that yet," Cathy purred as she came into the room. Head to foot in skin-tight leather, she looked them over with piercing eyes framed with a Cat Woman mask. Although red lipstick shaped the pouting mouth, the outfit tended to emphasise the masculine form beneath, with the wide shoulders and long arms making it appear ungainly and top-heavy.

Kyle bore the appraisal with as much dignity as he could. He had learned a long time ago not to make any attempts at modesty and waited with stomach-churning dread. He was aware of the heat from Sean's trembling body next to him.

Cathy twirled one finger in the air, and they turned around.

"Okay, face front." She pointed. "You, Kyle, isn't it? Do you work out?"

"I use the gym and run when I can."

Her eyes widened. "Bill lets you do that, does he?" Kyle didn't know how to respond. "He must trust you." Her gaze slid to Sean. "I can see you don't exercise much, boy, but you're pretty in your own way. Do you fuck each other?"

"No, ma'am," Sean said as Kyle shook his head.

Her red mouth stretched into an unpleasant smile. "There's always a first time." She licked her lips. "Okay. Let's get down to it." She picked up an object which made Kyle flinch in anticipatory fear. "You, fairy boy, come here." She pointed a riding crop at Sean. "Come here, boy. I won't mark you. I'm a Dom. I know what I'm doing."

Sean took a nervous step forward.

Kyle looked between the fear-filled face and the salacious grin. In his head, something snapped like a rubber band, and he flung an arm across Sean's chest. "No."

"What's going on?" Cathy said. "Let him go."

"No."

Sean gasped and grabbed his arm.

For a moment, Cathy looked confused, then her face cleared as if she understood. "You jealous, little man? You wanna be first?"

"Fuck. Off."

"What . . . what did you say?"

A calm confidence flooded Kyle. "I said, fuck off, you sleazy bastard. You're not beating either of us. We don't deserve it." The more he spoke, the stronger he felt. At one level, he was aware that the person with the whip would win, but at another, he felt a heady sense of liberation.

Cathy's expression was incredulous. She was tapping the whip against her thigh. Her voice became low and rough. "Have you any idea, you stupid wee prick, what Bill will do to you when I tell him about this?"

"Don't care." Kyle heard his voice tremble.

Sean was pulling against his arm. "It's okay, Kyle," he mumbled. "I can take it."

"You don't have to. He's no more a Dom than I am. He just likes hurting people."

The parts of the face not hidden by the mask blushed scarlet.

Sick with terror, Kyle tensed for action.

Without warning, she bounded forward, whip raised to strike.

Sean screamed.

Somehow, Kyle found himself running. Adrenaline powered through him, swamping fear. They collided. The whip glanced off his shoulder. Alcohol-smelling spittle sprayed from Cathy's mouth as she grunted and swore. They struggled, and Kyle quickly realised he was outmatched. In desperation, he jerked his knee upwards into the groin.

A howl of pain and long masculine hands clutched between leather-clad legs as Cathy staggered back, teetering on high heels. Tripping backwards on a barbell, she floundered with arms wide and mouth gaping until with a great clanking thud, she landed on the floor-plate of the running machine and lay still.

Chapter Five

Shoulder to shoulder, they stood staring.

Kyle moved first. Sean grabbed his hand as he tiptoed over to Cathy's prone form. The back of the head rested on the edge of the machine footplate.

Blood dripped into an ever-growing pool of red, shocking in its intensity against the white floor. The wig's hair was sticking up in two bloody tufts like horns, and the eyes behind the mask were fixed and staring. It was grotesque. An eyelid twitched. Kyle flinched back dragging Sean with him.

"Is she dead?" Sean whispered.

"I don't know."

"We have to check the pulse."

"How?"

"One of us has to touch her."

Kyle wrinkled his nose and recoiled. "On you go, then."

"Why can't you?"

"I don't know what to do."

"I don't either really. Just shagged a doctor once and he sort of showed me."

There was a thunderous crash, and they both leapt into the air. The Saint Andrew's cross lay on the floor; one broken leg stretched across Cathy's chest.

"Thank God I wasn't on that. I'd have been squashed like a tomato," Sean whispered in the silence.

With a nervous giggle, Kyle stepped forward and stared hard at Cathy's eyes. No twitch.

Sean crouched over the body and fumbled at its neck. "Nothing," he said straightening. "No pulse."

Taking a deep breath, Kyle stretched out his right foot and nudged a hand, splayed as if reaching for the whip. No movement. He did it again, stamping hard. The hand jerked and stilled.

"She's dead." Sean's voice rose. "They'll think we killed her. Oh my God."

Terror of the consequences clamped an icy grip on Kyle's stomach, and he struggled not to throw up.

"What are we going to do?" Sean wailed, his eyes filling with tears. "She was Bill's pal. We've had it. Oh God, what have we done?"

"*We* haven't done anything, it was me, and I didn't kill her. It was an accident."

"Why did you fight her?" Sean sobbed, pretty face drawn and ugly with fear, mascara trailing down his cheeks. "She had the right."

"No, she didn't, not to beat us up."

Sean wasn't listening. "Why didn't you just let her? She would have thumped us and shagged us. We've had all that before."

Kyle was silent. He didn't know why either. He just knew that he had reached a point of no return.

Dressed again, they hunted around the huge, state of the art kitchen and threw various edibles into a rucksack Kyle had found in a downstairs cupboard. He'd also found two heavy, waterproof jackets which he also purloined.

"Cans of coke here," Sean said as he explored a recess near the door.

"Just a couple," Kyle said from where he raided a cupboard. "Water would be better . . . and crisps, tins, stuff that'll keep." A phone rang somewhere in the house, and he paused, expecting someone to answer it. "What time is it, d'you think?"

"Don't know," Sean said, waving at the kitchen window. "But it's getting light. Where can we go? There's nowhere to hide." He glanced around, his gaze desperate.

The realisation that, despite his terror, he had to take responsibility for them both, hit Kyle hard. He took a deep breath. "We'll have to live rough for a bit until the furore dies down."

"The what?"

"The craziness that's going to happen when they find her body."

"They'll look for us, Kyle. They'll hunt us down," Sean said between sobs.

Kyle went over to him where he stood looking helpless, a can of coke in each hand. "Listen, Sean. You need to catch a grip here. Bubbling isn't helping either of us." He caught Sean's desperate gaze with his own and tried to instil some courage from his depleted supply. "We're going to get through this."

After a moment, Sean wiped his nose with the back of his hand, nodded and hugged him. They trembled in unison.

"So, this is what we're going to do," Kyle said, making it up as he went along. "We'll take a couple of duvets, roll them up in plastic bags and use them as beds. We'll head for Glasgow 'cause I know my way around."

"But that's where Bill is," Sean started to argue. He looked at Kyle and busied himself with packing.

"That's why he'll never think to look for us there. Anyway, we can make our base under the motorway where the homeless people live. We can have a fire and heat up tins of beans and soup. Then, when the coast is clear, we can go to the police."

"Will they be friendly?"

"Who, the police?"

"No, the homeless people."

"Sure they will." Kyle worked at sounding reassuring. "There's always homeless people in cities. They're bound to help each other out."

Chapter Six

Standing in line for a hand-out, Kyle's own words came back to haunt him.

He looked at Sean, ghostly pale and shivering, racked by a cough which made him clutch his chest and wheeze. Neither of them had their thick jackets. They had gone, along with almost everything else by their third night of living rough. Since then, he had slept only fitfully, watching over Sean, who grew more fragile every day. Virtual starvation led to Kyle giving in to the inevitable. The men had hurt him badly, scattering money and laughingly urinating on him as they left, but it enabled him to buy some food and a hot drink for Sean.

The woman in the Homeless Aid van who was distributing out-of- date sandwiches and tea seemed to look down her nose at them.

Sean burst into a fit of coughing, and she paused, brow crinkling slightly. "Are you alright?" she asked.

"He's fine," Kyle said, stuffing the food in his pockets and taking a plastic cup of tea.

She turned away. "Hello, Jimmy. You still here then? When are you off to Aberdeen?"

Kyle didn't hear the reply as he helped Sean over to the wall next to the Railway Station, where he collapsed. Kyle pulled off his own damp hoodie and tucked it around Sean's shaking shoulders. "Here, drink it while it's hot," he said, supporting him to sit upright.

Sean tried, broke into another coughing fit and pushed it away. "Take your jumper back. You'll freeze," he said when he'd caught his breath. "I'm fine."

Kyle held the cup so Sean could sip from it. "We need to find a doctor."

Usually, Sean argued, but this time he just sat there, wheezing.

Helpless in the face of his need, Kyle pulled him close and gently rocked him.

Gradually, the wheezing calmed somewhat and the shivering reduced. People walked to and from the station entrance. A warm draft of air hit them each time the doors opened, and Kyle began to drift into a doze. Sean's whisper woke him.

"If I die . . .

"You aren't going to die." Kyle pulled him closer.

"But if I do, I want you to know I love you." Sean broke into another coughing bout.

"Is your friend ill, son?" a woman's voice asked.

Startled, Kyle looked up to a friendly, smiling face, reminding him of someone from the past that he couldn't remember. He felt tears prick his eyes. "He . . . he has flu or something. He can't stop coughing."

The woman had white hair and looked well off. She crouched before them and touched Sean's face with the back of her knuckles. She smelt of flowers. "Swing the brolly here, Maisie," she said over her shoulder to another woman, waiting in the rain.

Kyle watched in concern as she cradled Sean's head between her hands and whispered to him. He opened his mouth, and she peered within, laying a hand flat on his chest. Sean began his great, wrenching coughs again, tears streaming down his face.

"Take it easy," she said and pulled off a woollen shawl she had pinned over her coat. When she wrapped it around him he grabbed it with both trembling hands. "Maisie, phone an ambulance. Say it's me and we need it urgent." She turned to Kyle. "And you, young man. Do you have the flu too?"

Kyle shook his head, dizzy with lack of sleep. "I'm fine."

"You don't look fine. How long have you been sleeping rough?"

Kyle tried to remember. "Two or three weeks, I think." He blinked up at the gathering onlookers and froze. Impaled by the piercing gaze, he struggled to his knees.

"What is it? What's wrong?"

"Got to go, we've got to go." Kyle grabbed Sean's arm and stared at the crowd. For an instant he was there, tall and blond.

Sean began coughing again.

"He needs the hospital," the woman insisted. "I'm a doctor. He's very ill."

"You don't understand," Kyle began and looked again at the small crowd. No sign of him. He stared around, wondering if he had imagined it.

An ambulance drew up to the pavement, scattering the crowd.

<>

Spike watched from a doorway as Sean was carried into the ambulance. Kyle didn't look much better as he stumbled, clutching a blanket around himself.

The city search was on the point of being called off, and it was a fluke to discover them as he headed home for the night. From what he glimpsed while the old woman was examining Sean, both boys looked exhausted and ill, but this would cut no ice with Bill. Despite the police reporting no apparent evidence of foul play, Bill wanted an explanation for Cathy's death. She was an old friend and, more importantly, a good customer, whose death was bad for business. Putting aside any feelings of liking or even affection which had developed through familiarity with the boys, Spike pulled out his mobile and reported in.

Chapter Seven

Still clutching the blanket given to him by the ambulance medic, Kyle stood outside the treatment room where they'd taken Sean. The window was partly obscured by something stuck to the other side, but he could make out figures in green moving around a trolley. One of the figures detached itself and pushed through the swing doors. Kyle looked up into the sculptured features of a tall, black nurse.

"Hi, I'm Stuart, the Senior Charge Nurse. Are you with Sean?"

"Yes, how is he?"

"He's quite ill. He has a deep-seated chest infection which needs to be treated in the High Dependency Unit." Stuart went on to ask questions about Sean

Despite sharing a flat for two years, Kyle knew very little about Sean and wouldn't have said if he did know. "He's eighteen, that's all I know. Sorry. Can I see him?"

"Not for a while yet," Stuart said, gaze flicking over Kyle's face. "What about you? You don't look so good either." His dark brows creased as he gently pulled down Kyle's left eyelid.

Kyle flinched and stepped back. "I'm fine."

Stuart tipped his head to one side and a smile illuminated his handsome face. "Are you hungry, son?"

As if in response Kyle's stomach growled, and Stuart grinned.

"Tell you what. I'm due a break soon. I'll pick up something from the canteen. Bacon rolls ok?"

Saliva rushed into Kyle's mouth and he nodded, dizzy at the thought. As the tall, dark figure disappeared back through the swing doors, Kyle found a seat in the busy waiting area. Sometime later, he was wakened by Stuart carrying a takeaway carton and coffee. He almost fainted at the smell.

"I think I can find you somewhere a bit more private." Stuart smiled.

Kyle warily followed the coffee smell to a room out of the way of the main area with a sign which Stuart slid to read 'Engaged.'

"You shouldn't be disturbed here," Stuart said, handing him the food and drink. "The toilets are just along the corridor there. I'll pop back later and let you know how Sean is."

Kyle mumbled his thanks before falling on the food like a starving dog. Afterwards, he felt sick and his stomach hurt, but determined not to throw up, he lay down on a couch and fell into a dreamless sleep.

When he woke again, he found a packet of sandwiches, crisps and two bottles of water laid on the couch opposite, together with a pile of clothing. Without questioning the source, he gulped down one bottle and kept the other for later, before polishing off the food. In the clothing pile there were jeans, t-shirt and jumper, a thick jacket, socks and even underwear, all worn but clean. Astonished at the kindness of strangers, he stripped off and changed. The jeans were too big, but he rolled them over the top of his belt and slid the pen drive inside his sock, before stuffing his dirty clothes into a waste bin.

After locating the toilets, he used the facilities, took his time washing his hands until the two other men had left and quickly pulled off his upper clothes. He washed himself with liquid soap, sluicing off with warm tap water, then quickly dropped his trousers and washed his lower half. He used the soap to wash his hair, scrubbing out the weeks of filth until the water ran almost clean and dried it as best he could by crouching under the hand dryer. Dressed again and feeling like a new man with the warm jacket fastened securely around him, he took a deep breath before venturing into the busy waiting area. He walked quickly through the noisy throng of people, and glanced at a huge wall clock decorated with cartoon characters, registering 15.00. Surprised that he had slept so long, he carried on to A & E.

"Stuart?" a nurse replied, when he enquired. "He's on night shift. Won't be back until tonight. Can I help?"

"I need to find out about someone. He was in here yesterday. Stuart said he was moving somewhere else."

"He'll have been moved yesterday, then. Do you know where to?"

"I think he said Intensive Care."

"That's one floor up, but you probably won't get in to see him," she said. "You could ask at Reception, though. If you're family, they might give you an update."

After several wrong turns through the maze of corridors, he saw an arrow pointing to INTENSIVE CARE. The doors were plastered with stickers warning to be quiet and to press for assistance. He reached for the buzzer.

"Hello, Kyle," said a familiar voice.

With a gasp of terror, he spun around and froze.

"Fancy meeting you here," Spike said with a smile. "If you're looking for Sean, he's next door in what they call HDU. Not doing very well, they tell me."

Kyle was transfixed, his tongue felt too big for his mouth. He watched Spike shove his hands into his coat pockets and tried to calculate how he could get past him.

"How're you doing anyway?" Spike enquired. "We've been worried."

At the other end of the corridor, behind Spike's back, Kyle could see lift doors opening and a trolley being trundled in their direction. He found his voice. "We didn't kill her. It was an accident."

Spike smiled again. "We know that."

The trolley was gaining on them. "She tripped and fell," Kyle said.

"Sure she did." Spike nodded. "Bill isn't angry with you. You ran off because you were scared, but it's time to come home now." He held out a hand. "You know he likes you."

Kyle stepped forward as if to take his hand.

The trolley reached Spike. "Excuse me, sir," said one of the porters.

As Spike turned, Kyle walked quickly past him, breaking into a run and heading for the stairs. Two flights down, heart pounding, he looked up and saw the brush of Spike's coat and his long legs taking the stairs two at a time.

"Kyle, stop." Spike's voice echoed.

On the ground floor, Kyle halted, staring wildly at three branching corridors. There were no signs in evidence. He dashed along the first one.

"No-one's going to hurt you. We just want you to come home." Spike's voice was closer.

Kyle was sweating and beginning to gasp for breath, and his heart was hammering so hard he could feel it against his ribs. Three weeks living rough had done nothing for his fitness.

The dark corridor had a cold and dismal feel and with no thought other than escape, he pushed open the nearest door and slid through. The room was cold but with his movement, lights flickered on. He could see sinks and trollies, and he crouched behind one, trembling with fear.

The door remained closed, and he began to breathe easier and get himself under control. He was aware of a sweetish, rotting smell like a forgotten kitchen bin.

Not for one instant did he believe Spike. He was Bill's creature, through and through. Kyle had witnessed how Bill welcomed people home and Spike had been one of his tools of retribution.

Warily, he stood up, almost leaping in the air as an electrical noise like a freezer chugging to life, broke the silence. A chemical smell wafted past, making his nose itch and his eyes water. He needed to sneeze and slapped both hands over his nose to muffle it. As he blinked in the dim light, he glanced at what lay on the trolley. A grey face with eyes rolled back and mouth gaping open. With a squeal, he flinched back, slid on something and fell to his knees. When he touched the floor to steady himself, his fingers were wet. Convinced that it was bodily fluid, he retched and scrubbed his hands on his jeans.

A door opened. He froze. He heard the squeaking of rubber-soled shoes. He crawled under the trolley, trembling from head to foot. The footsteps grew closer and paused.

In desperation, he looked across at the door, judging the distance to run. Spike was tall, with long legs. He'd catch him easily. The footsteps again, but moving away. Holding his breath, he crawled on hands and knees to the door and gently slid into the corridor. For a few seconds he crouched there and peered around, before creeping along the wall to the end.

The double doors were marked 'Mortuary Personnel Only' and swung outwards.

He found himself in a large yard, with a shelter for trollies at one side and at the other, an open gateway leading to a road. At the gate stood Spike, phone at his ear.

As Spike raised his head and looked straight at him, a man in the trolley shelter shouted, "That door's private."

With a gasp Kyle turned back and tried to push the doors open.

"Get away from there," the man bawled.

He scrabbled between them, breaking his nails, when a hand grabbed him by the scruff of the neck and pulled him away. In desperation, Kyle struggled and kicked out, making contact with a leg.

Spike swore and slapped him. He reeled, gasping for breath.

"Hey, you! Leave that boy alone."

"Mind your own business," Spike spat.

"This is my business. I'm Security. Let him go, or I'll call the police."

"Now, there's no need for that. He's my son."

"No, I'm not," Kyle gasped.

"Let him go!" the man yelled as a second security man ran towards them. "Come over here, son."

Spike's grip relaxed and heart thrashing in his ears, Kyle took off on shaky legs for the open gate.

Half aware of the raised voices behind him, he ran onto the hospital access road, dodging cars and pedestrians alike. He risked a glance behind. Spike was in pursuit. Kyle pushed himself on, past the ancient Cathedral and the Museum of Religion and downhill on to the High Street. He was out of condition. His breathing was laboured, and his legs felt heavier as he wound through tourists with cameras.

A black transit van screeched on to the pavement. The door slid open and a man leapt out, arms reaching for him.

With a yelp of fear, Kyle dodged into a narrow, cobbled street and kept up a stumbling run. There was no traffic and above the sound of his own harsh breathing, he could hear pounding footsteps. Ahead, he could see traffic zooming along a busy road. The footsteps neared. *Can't stop.*

Chapter Eight

Aaron Douglas was tired. He'd had a busy shift trying to manage two wards, until the new admission had been brought in by the police, then it became manic. As usual, the police quickly dumped and left them to grapple with the young, psychotic man, convinced he was being attacked by demons. Two nurses had struggled with him until Aaron had piled on to administer the sedation. He had been elbowed in the ribs and kneed in the groin. It sometimes happened and no-one blamed the patient, but driving home, peering through the rain which had come from nowhere in a great deluge, his sore bits throbbed.

The street lights flickered on and off again, and lorries sped past, overwhelming his wipers with spray. He was leaning forward and swearing aloud, when a figure seemed to materialise in front of him. He stood on the brake pedal. The big four-wheel drive responded, but it was too late and the figure was flipped over the bonnet, arms and legs flailing and bounced off on to the road.

After a momentary shock, Aaron was out of the car, just missing being squashed by a bus, before kneeling on the wet, oily road beside the prone victim. Aware of someone sheltering them with an umbrella, he began with infinite care to check vital signs. Blood pooled beneath the victim's head as he bent closer to check his pulse. An exploratory glance confirmed a compound fracture to the left leg, which was spurting blood and lying at a crooked angle.

"Is he dead?" asked someone.

"I saw it happen," another voice chimed in. "He just ran in front of the car."

"He's alive," Aaron said over his shoulder. "Has anyone phoned an ambulance?"

The victim was unconscious, but he was young and his pulse was strong. Concerned about a possible neck injury, Aaron glanced around. "I need help here."

A man dropped to a crouch beside him. "I've had first aid training."

Aaron glanced at him. "Do you know how to support his head until he gets a collar on?"

"Sure." The man crawled across and cradled the boy's head between his hands.

Once he was satisfied it was being done correctly, Aaron focussed on the bent and bleeding left leg. To his relief, he heard an ambulance warning traffic to get out of its way.

"Compound fracture?" his helper asked.

Aaron nodded and glanced at him. He was a good-looking man with the high cheekbones and firmly shaped lips of a model. His hair was pale and so plastered to his head by the rain that it looked like a skull.

After relaying the situation to the ambulance medics, Aaron backed off to let them do their job. He glanced around to thank his helper, but he was gone.

<>

The Accident and Emergency waiting area was busy as usual, and Aaron noticed several hopeful eyes fixed on Stuart as he crouched before him.

"Are you okay?" the ebony eyes were filled with concern.

"I'm fine, Stu, I'm here with a patient."

"Which patient? I thought you were finishing at five tonight?"

"Tried to. I ran someone over outside the back entrance," Aaron said, only now allowing himself to feel the shock of it.

Stuart blinked, then understanding dawned. "The young man with the compound fracture?"

Aaron nodded. "How is he?"

"Gone to theatre. Are you okay?"

Aaron shrugged. "Bit shaky."

His friend's face filled with concern. "Come on through."

"I'm fine," Aaron insisted, but followed him to the staffroom.

"Medics." Stuart shook his head and guided him into a comfy chair. "We think we're invincible." He cradled Aaron's face between his hands, his dark eyes filled with affection. "Hot drink, lots of sugar?"

"Aren't you busy?" Aaron smiled.

"On a break. I was on my way to the canteen when I saw you sitting there." Stuart began to busy himself with kettle and cups. "That boy was here last night with a friend, both homeless. I got him food from the canteen and put him in a family room to sleep. His friend's in HDU. Not a good prognosis."

Only half listening, Aaron scrubbed his hands across his face. "I can't understand why he did it."

"Who did what?" Stuart asked, handing him a steaming mug.

"The boy I hit. Why didn't he wait? He could have gone up to the lights and pressed the button. It's like he was running away from something."

"Have you seen the police yet?"

Aaron nodded. "At the scene." A thought occurred to him and he frowned at his friend. "Hang on, what're you doing here, anyway? Thought you were on nights?"

"Called in early. Half the shift's off with a bug." Stuart rolled his eyes.

A smiling, female nurse interrupted. "Stuart, you're needed."

Stuart nodded understanding. "Go home, Aro," he said, dropping his car keys on the coffee table. "I'll get a taxi."

Amazed that Stuart had trusted him with his pride and joy, Aaron slid into the luxurious interior of his E-type Jag. He took a moment to inhale the delicious smell of leather and adjusted the seat to allow for his longer legs. His mobile dinged a text message.

"Hi. Coming home sooner than I thought. Will let you know flight details. Sandi x"

As his wife had only returned from home leave a month ago, Aaron was surprised, then mentally shrugged. It was the army, after all. He sent her a quick acknowledgement, started the car and glanced in the mirror. A long coat swirling around his ankles, his helper from the accident was striding across the car park. "Hey, wait," he said, fumbling with the door handle. By the time he got out, the man had stepped into a waiting black van, which sped off in the opposite direction.

Chapter Nine

Consciousness was gradual. Kyle cracked open one eye. The room spun around him and a sour taste flooded his mouth. He closed it quickly and gulped for breath. He became aware of hushed voices and bleeping noises and blinked open his eye again. The spinning had stopped.

His other eye seemed to be stuck, and he raised a hand to pry it open. There was a thing on his forefinger and something stuck to the back of his hand. He heard himself moan.

"Hey there, Kyle, you're okay," said a disembodied voice. "You're in hospital. You've had a road accident, but you're fine. Just relax now." He drifted.

When he came to again the light was dimmer and he could hear squeaking. A mouse? He remembered, hospital, so it couldn't be a mouse. Lying on his back, so he must be in a bed. A needle in the back of his hand, hurting and itchy. He extended his awareness to the rest of his body. Everything ok until he got to his legs. Numb. He tried wiggling his toes. His right foot worked, but not his left. He couldn't feel his left leg. His breath caught. He began to feel the beginning of a panic attack. A vague memory surfaced that he'd been in an accident. Had he lost his leg? A sharp bleeping noise. The squeaking again.

"It's okay, Kyle." A woman's voice. "You're okay. You've had an operation, but you're fine."

Kyle heard her move around his bed, shoes squeaking as she walked.

"I've finished," a man said. "This one's gone. Increase that one's sedative."

A dark shutter came down.

In the morning, he discovered to his horror that Sean had died in the night.

Chapter Ten

When he arrived at the High Dependency Unit, Aaron was delighted to discover an old University friend in charge.

"How long have you been here, Darren?" He smiled as they exchanged hugs.

"Just started this week. Transferred from the Royal in London."

"Missing the Glasgow scene, huh?" Aaron grinned. "How's Gary?"

Darren's boyish face fell. "Gary and I split up four months ago."

"Aw, hell, I'm sorry."

"These things happen." Darren shrugged. "You still in mental health?"

Aaron nodded, before explaining the situation. "So, I feel a bit responsible for the lad and wondered if I could visit?"

"I don't see why not. He's just finished lunch and had his medication, so he might be a bit sleepy," Darren said, checking the computer. "I'll go ask him."

While he was gone and conscious of health and safety, Aaron pulled a gown on top of his scrubs and rubbed his hands with antiseptic.

"Told him you're the man who saved his life." Darren grinned on his return. "His name's Kyle, by the way."

As they walked through the ward, Darren leaned closer. "His friend died two nights ago, an embolism." Aaron nodded in concern. "He thinks someone killed him." Darren lowered his voice. "He has scars across his stomach and arms and he wakes up screaming during the night." He shrugged. "You'll know far better than me what that's all about."

Aaron took this into account when he saw the boy he'd last seen unconscious and bleeding on the road.

Kyle's damp hair shone dark red in the lights. It was brushed off his forehead revealing a gash sealed with medi-strips. He was good-looking, although his face was pale and drawn. He warily watched their approach with huge silver-grey eyes

"Hi, Kyle," Darren said. "This is Aaron Douglas."

Aaron nodded and smiled his greeting. The expression in the boy's eyes didn't change. "How're you feeling?"

"How d'you think? Are you a doctor?"

"No, I'm a nurse too." Aaron smiled, ignoring the hostility.

"I'll leave you to it, then." Darren smiled as he turned and left to walk back up the quiet ward.

"You certainly look better than when I last saw you," Aaron said, aware that the grey eyes were scrutinizing him from head to foot.

"You work here?"

"In this hospital, but not in this ward. D'you mind if I sit down?"

Kyle shrugged. "He said you saved my life."

Aaron grimaced. "Not exactly, and what he didn't tell you was that I ran you over first." As he adjusted the visitor's chair and sat, he caught the grey eyes widen. "Although, in my defence you did crash into me. Can you remember?"

Kyle shook his head and looked away.

"It's normal to have some memory loss after a trauma like that. You banged your head pretty hard so you'll—"

"Have a concussion," Kyle finished. "They told me." He looked at Aaron, his gaze penetrating. "Do you know when I can get out of here?"

"Not for a while yet. You'll be moved from here to an ordinary ward."

"When will that be?"

"Depends on how well you heal. Usually a few days to a week."

Kyle continued to stare as if checking whether he was telling the truth, then looked down at the bed clothes. He took a deep breath and slowly exhaled. "Can I get a private room?"

"I don't know," Aaron said, trying to figure him out. "Is that important?"

Kyle nodded his head.

"Why?"

The head shot up, eyes narrowed. "What's it to you? What're you doing here anyway? I didn't ask you to."

Aaron leaned back, palms held out flat in a conciliatory gesture. "Cool your jets, my friend. I'll leave anytime you want."

Kyle glared for a moment, then the light faded from his eyes and he looked back down at the bedding.

"I'm sorry about your friend," Aaron ventured. There was no response, and he prepared to leave.

"I thought he was murdered," Kyle said so quietly he had to strain to hear.

"Do you want to tell me about it?" Aaron asked, and Kyle did, talking to his clenched fists, while tears leaked from his closed eyelids and dripped down his cheeks.

Aaron listened to the halting tale of two homeless boys in the pitiless city streets in winter. Of one taking ill and the other not knowing what to do. Of one dying in hospital while the other lay helpless in the next bed.

When he was sure Kyle had finished, Aaron leaned forward and spoke in the gentle tone he used when supporting someone who was traumatised. "You sound like you cared about him a lot."

Kyle nodded. "But not as much as he cared about me," he whispered.

Aaron paused, but decided not to follow this up. "Why did you think he was murdered?" he asked in the same quiet tone.

Kyle sighed. "I woke up one night. The . . . the night he died. There was a woman telling me everything was alright. She was dressed like you." Kyle indicated Aaron's white robe. "I know why you have to wear it in here now, but then I didn't. And she had a mask over her face too. It was just weird." He half shrugged his thin shoulders. "There was a guy leaning over the next bed." Eyes full of hurt, he looked up at Aaron. "Didn't even know it was Sean's bed. He . . . he said, this one's gone."

"That was it? This one's gone?"

With an embarrassed shrug, Kyle looked away. "I was a bit out of it, but I'm not hallucinating."

"Course not. You'd have been disorientated and probably a bit scared." Aaron was surprised when Kyle looked at him and nodded as if he was understood. He watched him yawn and rub his eyes like a child. His bed was in a corner, curtains half drawn. All was quiet but for the gentle swish of life-support machines.

It was peaceful, like the moments Aaron had sometimes known in the tiny hospital chapel. He watched Kyle's face slacken and his breathing change. "Go to sleep now," he whispered. "You're safe here."

Groggily, Kyle lay back on his pillows, and Aaron tucked him in.

"Come back?" Kyle mumbled.

"I promise."

Chapter Eleven

When he had first moved into the orthopaedic ward, Kyle had felt more secure. It was just another ward within the many and he thought would be more difficult for anyone to find him.

As promised, Aaron had visited him regularly, depending on his work schedule. Once to take him by wheelchair to Sean's funeral service in the hospital chapel and hold his hand while he cried. Others, to bring him necessities like toothpaste and toiletries but often he also brought magazines, fruit and sometimes sweets. Kyle didn't know how to take this generosity. In his world, no-one did favours for nothing.

He was restless, and his frustration grew when his leg developed an infection which necessitated a longer stay. Aaron's visits did help. Twice he brought friends; Stuart, the nurse who'd been kind to him in A & E and Stuart's partner Dave, whose beard, clothing and cowboy boots, made him look like he should have been in a movie. At first, their presence was intimidating, but the three men treated him in such a natural, friendly way, including him in their banter and asking nothing of him, that he relaxed in their company. He stopped worrying why Aaron showed such an interest in him and began to look forward to seeing his tall figure striding down the ward towards him.

On the fourteenth day, everything changed.

"Have you remembered any more about the accident?" Aaron asked out of the blue. "Were you being chased?"

Kyle gazed at him, thoughts going a hundred miles an hour. He wanted to tell him, wanted to tell him everything, but he was afraid and ashamed. How could people living in their nice, clean worlds understand the foulness of his.

"I . . . I was running and couldn't stop," he finally admitted.

"Because you were being chased?" Aaron had the most open, friendly eyes Kyle had ever seen. An unusual shade of brown, they lit when he smiled, which was often, showing hints of amber.

Kyle gazed at him. Behind the curtain, the man in the next bed answered his mobile and complained about no-one bringing him cigarettes.

"Are you in trouble?" Aaron asked softly.

Still hooked by his eyes, Kyle nodded.

"Can you tell me?"

The visitors' bell rang, triggering raised voices, thundering feet and the scraping of chairs.

Aaron's eyes were now apologetic. "I'm sorry, I have to go," he said. "Didn't realise it was that time."

Kyle wanted to cry. "It's okay."

"I'll come back soon." And he was gone.

Kyle lay back against the raised pillows and closed his eyes. He felt relief and disappointment at the same time, and his leg throbbed.

"Hello, son. How are you?"

He opened his eyes. Spike stood beside his bed. Without conscious volition, Kyle shrank against the pillows.

Spike propped himself on the edge of the bed, shielding them from the visitors clustered around the next patient. "I'm sorry I haven't managed in before. You know how busy it gets in our line of work." He laid a carrier bag across Kyle's lap. "Your Uncle Bill says hello."

As if it was a crawling spider, Kyle shoved it off. A packet of sweets fell out. His stomach was clenched so hard it was sore. He was struggling to breathe. "Piss off," he managed to whisper.

In response, Spike patted his injured leg. "I know you're unhappy, son, but things will get better." He took a hold of Kyle's left hand in a tight grip, leaned forward and whispered in his ear, "You're just a whore, Kyle. And don't you forget it. A hole to fuck." He squeezed Kyle's hand hard, making him bite back a cry of pain and raised his voice. "We're all missing you, son."

Kyle tried to pull his hand free, but it was held as if in a vice. Spike spoke into his ear again. His breath warm and minty. "Bill's been good to you and he's ready to take you back, no questions asked, now Sean's dead." His gaze was meaningful.

Before Kyle could react, Spike stood up and dropped a folded newspaper on the bed. "See you soon," he said with a wink and walked off.

Kyle lay there, fighting to control his panic. It came with waves of shameful memories. He shook and sweated and wanted to die.

<>

The desperate expression in the boy's eyes stayed with Aaron all the way back to his own ward. It was against his nature and his training to abandon someone so clearly in need. Already late for his shift, he quickly changed into his uniform and hurried to the main office where his counterpart and friend, Caroline, was leading the shift changeover.

"Good evening, Mr Douglas," she said, poker face. "Glad you could join us."

Aaron knew her well and merely arched his eyebrows as he took a seat in the group of nurses. When she'd finished and the room emptied, he put on his most charming smile. "Carrie, could you cover for me for a couple of hours?"

"When?"

"Now. There's something I really need to do." He noticed the lines of tiredness in her face and felt guilty. "I'm sorry, you look knackered."

"Thanks for that, Aaron." She yawned and stretched her arms above her head. "I can always rely on you to make me feel good."

Her expression changed, making her look younger and mischievous. "I'll give you 'til five, but you owe me big time, honey." She winked.

"Anytime." He winked back in the game they played.

Chapter Twelve

Visitors were trickling back and forth from Kyle's ward. Aaron stepped to the side of the corridor to avoid a wheelchair and straight into the path of a hurrying figure. "I'm sorry . . ." He began to apologise as the man pushed past him. There was something familiar about the tall, lean figure with the pale hair.

"Excuse me," he called to the man's back.

The man turned around, eyebrows raised.

"I think you're the guy who helped me at the road accident," Aaron said. There was no flicker of recognition on the stony face. "With Kyle, the young guy with the compound fracture? Have you been to visit him?"

There was a subtle change in the man's expression. His eyes narrowed, and he made an abrupt departure, leaving Aaron to frown at his behaviour.

Back in the ward, at first, Aaron thought Kyle asleep, until he saw the fists tightly crushing a newspaper, the sweat soaked brow. Carefully, he crouched beside Kyle's trembling form. A quick assessment told him it wasn't a seizure he was witnessing, but an anxiety attack. He began to speak gently, until by the flicker of eyelids and change in breathing, he knew that Kyle was aware of his presence. "That's it, well done. Keep taking deep breaths."

"Had a row with his dad, I think," the man in the next bed said.

Aaron looked around. "His dad?"

The old man nodded and rolled his eyes. "Punky looking bloke, bit twitchy. You know what I mean?"

For Aaron, something fell into place. The fortuitous appearance of the man at the accident and the same man in the corridor; the apparent recognition of Kyle's name. It all seemed to add up. He turned back to Kyle and continued murmuring reassuring words. After a few moments Kyle began to relax, and Aaron mopped his face with tissues. "It's ok. You don't have to see him again if you don't want to."

Kyle gazed at him with wet eyes. "Wh-What?"

"Your dad," Aaron said quietly. "The tall, blond guy."

Kyle blinked as if coming out of a dream. "*He's* not my fucking dad," he muttered, scrubbing his hands over his face. "How . . . how do you know him?"

"Just saw him in the corridor. He helped at your accident."

Kyle looked shocked.

"You okay, son?" enquired the man in the next bed. "My kids fall out with me all the time." The visiting bell rang, and he was surrounded by people saying goodbye.

As Kyle looked on the edge of tears, Aaron slid the privacy curtain between the beds. "Is that guy something to do with the trouble you're in?" The nod was so slight he almost missed it. "Is it drugs? Or money?"

"Nothing like that. You wouldn't understand."

"I could try."

With a heavy sigh, Kyle looked away. "Nobody can help."

"There's always a way," Aaron said, propping himself on the edge of the bed. He noticed the crushed newspaper and picked it up. "There's a solution to every problem. It's just a question of finding it." He smoothed out the paper, glanced at Kyle and stopped. Kyle's gaze was fixed on it. His eyes were wide and he looked terrified. Aaron looked down at the picture. It was the head and shoulders of a man in a police dress-uniform. Above him the headline read, *Top Police Chief Found Dead.* He looked up into haunted eyes. The rattle of trollies filled the silence. "Why don't we go somewhere quieter for tea."

<>

"I've found him," Spike said into his mobile.

"Where?"

"Still in hospital, different ward."

"Can you get him out?" Bill asked.

Spike moved around the corner from the main entrance into a quiet garden area. Pyjama-clad smokers were dotted around on benches. A graffiti scrawled notice advised that this was a fresh air garden, and smoking wasn't allowed. "I'm working on it."

"Work harder," Bill snarled and cut the call.

Chapter Thirteen

"Aren't you due crutches soon?" Aaron asked, halting Kyle's wheelchair in a deserted area where drinks and snacks were available to patients and visitors.

"They're fitting me for them tomorrow and a support boot."

"Good." Aaron smiled. "More independence. D'you want a drink or crisps or something from the machine, seeing as you're missing your afternoon cuppa?"

Kyle shook his head and chewed on his lower lip.

Unsure where to begin, but not one to hold back, Aaron took a deep breath and asked the question uppermost in his mind. "Did you know the policeman in the paper?" He watched Kyle squeeze his eyes shut and chew harder. "If you keep doing that you'll break the skin." Kyle was silent. "Look, Kyle, I'm not here to judge you or to make you do anything or say anything you don't want to, but I can see you need help, and I seem to be the only one around at the moment." He waited.

Kyle shuffled in his chair, his hair flopping forward over his brow. He rubbed the thigh of his injured leg as if it hurt. His sigh seemed to come from his boots. "She . . . he was going to beat us up."

It was so not what Aaron was expecting. "Say that again."

"She was going to beat us up," Kyle repeated, raising his head and fixing Aaron with an intense stare. "With a whip. She . . . he said she's a Dominatrix, but real Doms aren't usually sadistic. At Halloween, she hurt Sean so badly he could hardly stand." The words poured out. "I said she didn't have the right. They're not supposed to hurt us as bad as that. So, I kneed her between the legs, and she fell and banged her head." He paused, eyes darting back and forth between Aaron's as if awaiting a reaction.

Careful to show no sign of judgement, Aaron asked, "Did she – He die?" Kyle nodded and looked down at the floor. "Transgender?" Aaron asked quietly.

Kyle shrugged. "Don't know, doubt it. Just liked dressing up, I reckon."

"Was this in a BDSM club?"

"No. We were hired . . . rented for the night." Kyle dropped his head. "For . . . for sex. Me and Sean." He swallowed hard. "I'm not a prostitute, or . . . or a rent boy." His voice was muffled, and Aaron had to strain to hear. "I never wanted to . . . to go with any of them. Except when I'm drunk or high, and then I don't give a fuck what happens."

Aaron looked down at the angry, vulnerable boy curled before him in the wheelchair. The protective instinct which was so much a part of him roared to life. "Kyle," he said urgently, dropping to a crouch before the chair. "Does the blond guy know about this? Is that why he's after you?"

"That's part of it." Kyle paused and tossed his head as if he had long hair. His gaze when he looked up reflected a depth of pain that took Aaron's breath away. "He wants me back in the fold."

Aaron sat on a plastic bench beside him. "Do you want to tell me about it?" Long experience had taught him how to keep his own feelings under control when listening to disclosures, but sometimes it was difficult. He struggled as he listened to the horrifying story of an orphan boy, alone in the world, forced to survive in a residential school where children were systematically sexually abused.

"No-one could help?" Kyle whispered.

"Your social worker?"

Kyle snorted and shook his head. He rubbed his nose with the back of his knuckles as if it was itchy. "She hardly spoke to me."

"And when you were older?"

Kyle's face hardened. "Then I became one of the lucky ones." He shuddered, mouth twisting with the memory. "We had to perform at Bill's parties," he stammered, "G-go with different men." His chin came up, eyes flashing a challenge. "D'you believe me?"

"I believe every word." Aaron held Kyle's gaze with his own. "And not one bit of it was your fault." He watched tears spring to

Kyle's eyes. He felt like hugging him, but knew it wouldn't be appropriate. "Who is this Bill?"

"He runs the school. It's a charity. He's on the board and he makes sure perverts like him get jobs there." Kyle scrubbed at his eyes. "He also buys and sells kids for sex. Moves them around. He's got contacts all over the place. And he's a local councillor."

Aaron was appalled.

"I've had to work in his office for the last two years," Kyle said glancing at him, then he looked away. "Though I've still had to do other things."

"This sick fuck is a councillor?"

Kyle snorted. "Didn't think nurses knew words like that."

"You need to go to the police."

"No way."

Aaron leaned towards him. "Kyle, this bastard needs to be stopped."

Eyes resolute, Kyle shook his head. "No police."

"So, what are you going to do?"

Kyle shrugged and shook his head. "Dunno. Go on the run." He raised his head and gasped in shock. "Jesus."

Aaron followed his gaze and jumped to his feet as Spike strode towards them.

"Ok, Kyle you're coming with me," Spike said as he reached them. He made a grab for the wheelchair. Aaron knocked his hand away and stepped in front of it.

"You're not taking him anywhere."

"Leave it, Aaron. He'll hurt you," Kyle yelled.

"He's right, Aaron," Spike sneered his name.

Aaron held his ground, and the man's cold gaze. Spike was a couple of inches taller and probably well able to handle himself in a fight, but Aaron was absolutely determined to protect Kyle.

Spike's lip curled. "Get the fuck out of my way." His tone was contemptuous.

"Make me."

"Don't hurt him, Spike. Please don't hurt him," Kyle begged.

Recalling his University boxing days, Aaron watched Spike's eyes. When they flickered, he ducked to one side and landed a solid punch to the man's jaw. Spike went down like a sack of potatoes.

"Hey, what's going on?" a porter shouted, leaving the nearest lift with a patient-laden trolley.

"Call security," Aaron shouted back. He massaged his sore knuckles as he watched Spike scrabble to his knees, then to his feet.

For a moment Spike hesitated. "You'll pay for that," he promised, glaring at Aaron. "And you, you little shit—" At the sound of running footsteps, he took off towards the stairway.

Aaron turned around to find Kyle gazing at him in awe. "Are you alright?" Aaron asked him as two security officers thundered to a halt beside them.

"What's happening? Who was that guy?"

"Phone the police," Aaron instructed without taking his eyes off Kyle. He raised an eyebrow, and after a pause, Kyle nodded. "A man tried to kidnap this patient."

Chapter Fourteen

Kyle shuffled around in the wheelchair trying to ease the pressure on his hip.

"Are you ok, Kyle?" the female police officer asked in concern. "Are you due pain killers, or d'you need a drink?" She had introduced herself as Jen and had been solicitous of him from the outset. P.C. Andy Coyle, her male colleague, while taking the matter as seriously, had chosen to stand guard at the office door and communicate with colleagues.

"It's this chair," Kyle explained. "It's not designed for comfort." He still felt shaken from the scene with Spike and wished Aaron would get back before what Jen had called M.I.T. arrived. He had no idea what this was and his imagination was running riot. Was Robocop about to burst through the doors?

Jen's plain, no-nonsense face split into a grin. "Just you tell me anything you need."

The door opened, and Andy appeared. "They're on their way," he said to Kyle, then looked at Jen with a puzzled frown. "D.C.I. Jones?"

"Who's D.C.I. Jones?" Kyle asked, nervous about their silent communication.

"She's a highly respected and very experienced senior officer," Jen replied in a reassuring tone.

Not convinced and about to ask further questions, Kyle was relieved when Aaron appeared. He'd changed out of his uniform and wore a navy tee-shirt and jeans, although his hospital I.D. still hung around his neck. He smiled at Kyle and immediately, Kyle felt safer.

"My shift's covered and your ward staff know where you are." Aaron looked at Jen. "I've arranged a conference room to be available for the interviews."

"Great, thanks." Jen smiled and moved to the door to speak to Andy.

"How're you doing?" Aaron propped himself on the desk next to Kyle.

"Scared. How's your hand?"

Aaron grinned. "Fine, a bit stiff." He flexed it, and Kyle could see the muscles jump in his forearm and his swollen knuckles. "Don't be scared. You're well protected now." He pulled a rolled-up sock from his jeans pocket and handed it to Kyle.

Just holding it helped Kyle feel less helpless. "Thanks, but what if this is useless to them?" He buried his fingers in the soft wool and pulled out the pen-drive. "They won't believe me."

Aaron leaned forward. "I believe you. Why shouldn't they?"

Kyle looked up at him; the kindness in his eyes, his solid frame and had a sudden, confusing desire to be hugged against his chest.

"Hey," Aaron said quietly. "You're okay."

"They're here," Jen said.

<>

A short time later, Kyle was in a much more comfortable chair Aaron had brought from somewhere, with a blanket around him and his leg propped on a footstool. He'd had food, antibiotics and painkillers, and felt a bit drowsy as voices swirled around him.

"Are you alright?" Aaron asked, crouching beside him.

Before Kyle could reply, Detective Chief Inspector Jones joined them. "Your information is amazing," she said without preamble, hooking over a chair with one booted foot and sitting on it. "Names, dates, locations and all linking back to Fitchett. How did you manage to record so much?"

Kyle shrugged. "He trusted me." A momentary pang of guilt made him pause. "I told you I worked in his office."

She pushed a lock of dark brown hair behind her ear and nodded. "You're a Godsend," she said, including Aaron in her smile. "The Sexual Offences team has been trying to get something that will stick on the councillor for years, then you come along with evidence that he can't dispute. With that and your own testimony—"

"Hang on," Aaron interrupted. "Are you saying that Kyle is going to have to testify in court?"

She frowned and glanced between them. "Well, yes, we need his—your witness testimony to back-up the pen-drive."

"And just how are you going to keep him safe once all this gets out?"

With a star,t Kyle woke from his drowsiness. "What?"

"You'll have police protection while you're in hospital," she said, all business. "And when you're discharged, we'll move you to a safe house."

"Safe house?" Kyle repeated, out of his depth. He looked at Aaron who nodded and patted his forearm.

"To start with, let's get you settled in your own room, ok?"

<>

Once he understood what a safe house was, Kyle was determined not to go. The thought of living somewhere miles away, for who knew how long was terrifying.

"It's a very nice house." The policewoman had tried to encourage him. "Has a lovely garden and all the mod cons, including Wi-Fi as long as you're careful how you use it and you won't be alone."

"Yes, you said, police officers on shifts," Kyle muttered. "Just like jail."

She sighed and stood back as he hobbled to the bathroom.

"It's for your protection, just like in here." He heard her say as he closed the door, propped his crutch against the wall and hopped to the toilet. When he came out, Aaron had arrived and was leaning against the wall, listening to her. He smiled and winked at Kyle who immediately felt less alone.

"I've been trying to explain to Kyle that the police officers are there to protect him," she said, "but he's—"

"Kyle knows exactly what you mean," Aaron interrupted. "And he's been very clear that he's not going into a Safe House." He pushed himself off the wall and steadied Kyle into his chair, before taking the crutch and laying it over the bed. "And all this protection might not have been necessary if you hadn't leaked information to the papers."

Kyle gazed at him in shock.

"I did no such thing," she denied, her pale cheeks glowing red.

"Well, someone did," Aaron said, sitting on the edge of Kyle's bed.

"What d'you mean?" Kyle asked, looking from one to the other. "What's going on?"

"Would you care to tell him?" Aaron asked her. "Or shall I?"

His stomach churning, Kyle glared at Aaron. "Tell me what?"

Aaron sighed and pulled a rolled-up newspaper from the inside of his leather jacket. He straightened it and handed it to Kyle.

The tabloid headlines screamed from the front page:

LOCAL POLITICIANS IN CHILD ABUSE PROBE

With a growing sense of horror Kyle read the article.

Police investigating claims of child sex abuse in two local residential schools and three children's homes, have identified 46 Scottish VIPs, including politicians, TV, radio personalities and people from the world of sport.

The figures were revealed by a police spokesman and relate to Operation Undertow, a UK wide group set up by the National Police Chiefs' Council to investigate links between child sex abuse, child trafficking and 'prominent public persons.'

Detectives say that an ex-resident of Bakersville, a residential school for boys run by a charity, claims that boys as young as 8 have been drugged and abused there.

The Police continued, 'We have a number of live investigations which are ongoing and which would be wrong to comment on at this stage'. However, they agreed that victims of these horrific crimes should no longer suffer in silence and when they have the courage to come forward they must get the support they need. Our police spokesman promised that any witnesses who wish to come forward will be treated in strict confidence.

A spokesperson from the NSPCC said that the Jimmy Saville scandal had led to a surge in reports of abuse.

Kyle looked at the policewoman. "That's me, they're talking about me," he almost yelled. "An ex-resident. You told *me* everything I told you was in confidence."

"And it is, Kyle," she said, flapping her hands to try and calm him down. "I didn't authorise any statement to the press. I'm investigating the source."

Aaron cleared his throat. "According to your old boss, Dave Brand, this is called a fishing expedition, Inspector." He looked at Kyle. "Remember Dave? Stuart's partner? He used to be a policeman. He suggested this is a deliberate leak to encourage more witnesses to come forward."

With a sense of rising anxiety Kyle turned to the woman. "Why didn't you tell me . . . ask me? Don't you understand? He'll know it's me."

Her face scarlet, the policewoman rounded on Aaron. "You shouldn't have shown him the paper."

"He's not a child. He has a right to know."

They argued as Kyle struggled to breathe. The dizziness began and he squeezed his eyes shut, clutched his knees and fought against it. "Panic attack," he heard someone say. Then, all he was conscious of was the terror.

He slowly came around, to the sound of Aaron murmuring in his ear and a wonderful coolness on his face and neck.

"Keep taking big breaths," Aaron said. "Slowly in two, three, out two three. Remember the breathing technique I taught you."

Kyle opened his eyes. They were alone in the small room. Aaron knelt in front of him, supporting his upper body with one hand while he mopped his face with a damp cloth.

His eyes lit up. "Hey there, welcome back. Lost you there for a few minutes. Are you okay?"

Disorientated, Kyle blinked as Aaron gently pushed him upright. "What happened?" The memory returned. "Oh fuck."

"Now don't you go off again. Stay cool." Aaron sat back on his heels and reached for a water bottle on the night stand. He unscrewed the top and handed it to Kyle.

As if there was no tomorrow, Kyle gulped the lot. Anxiety attacks and nightmares always seemed to leave him feeling thirsty. Aaron had told him that his body was reacting in a normal way for someone who'd been through what he had. He'd also said that he could be helped to overcome the memories, but they hadn't talked about how. As he calmed, he remembered the safe house. "Can she make me go to this house?" he asked and felt relieved when Aaron immediately shook his head.

"No one can make you do anything you don't want to any longer," Aaron said, fetching him another bottle of water from the tiny fridge. He sat on the bed again, watching Kyle with a concerned expression. "You're due for discharge, and in normal circumstances you'd be assessed by a social worker and probably placed in a hostel."

"No way." Kyle was adamant.

"But, these aren't normal circumstances." Aaron paused. "So I have an idea, which you can also refuse." He paused again as Kyle waited expectantly. "I live in the country and have a spare room which you're very welcome to use until you get back on both feet."

Kyle felt his heart surge in his chest. "But . . . but what about your wife?"

"I think I mentioned Sandi's an army nurse. She's hardly ever home." Aaron shrugged. "I'm sure she'll be fine about it anyway, and Stuart stays when he's on shifts. When he's off, he goes down to the house he shares with Dave on the coast. The only other person who sometimes stays is my sister Evie." He waited, eyebrows arched.

Kyle was trying to keep his excitement under control. He felt he should say something sensible. "I . . . I don't have any money . . . I mean, I couldn't pay you rent."

Aaron waved a dismissive hand. "Not a problem. You can owe me if you want. When you're ready, you can register with the DSS, and you'll be able to claim criminal compensation."

Unable to keep it in, Kyle let his feelings show with a grin. "Cool, I mean, thanks."

Aaron grinned back. "That's the first time I've seen you smile properly." He laughed. "Let's make plans."

Chapter Fifteen

Kyle glanced at the clock and started in surprise. He'd been lying on the couch reading the whole afternoon. It was luxury, like having a whole bedroom to himself, with a bed that could fit three people in. When Aaron had first shown him the room, he'd wandered around with his mouth open. A TV fixed to the wall; a DVD player and X-Box; an en-suite bathroom, all in what Aaron called his spare room. He'd had more than a few shaky moments the first night he'd stayed, as he'd lain in his huge bed in the old house, with an unlocked door between Aaron in the next room and Stuart along the hall. It was blowing a gale outside, and there were ominous cracks and creaks which sounded like doors opening and closing. Old fears crept up. He and Nathan lying rigidly in their beds, waiting for their door to open and the voice—*Get up, you're needed.*

Unable to bear it any longer, he'd leapt out of bed and shoved a chair under the door handle, before he'd dived back under the duvet.

The next morning, seeing Aaron tousled and smiling in his dressing gown at the breakfast table, made him wonder what all the fuss was about.

"Did you sleep alright?" Aaron asked, pouring him some orange juice. "It was a wild night, and this house does a lot of groaning."

Kyle nodded and reached for a slice of toast.

"Yeah, it's not easy trying to get used to a new place." Aaron continued. "Especially one in a village in the middle of nowhere." He took a pensive sip of coffee. "So, I was thinking, if you need a lock on your door, I'll have one installed."

Kyle stopped buttering his toast and stared in astonishment.

"On the other hand, we don't have to."

"You'd do that? For me?"

"Of course, you're my guest," Aaron said and filled both their mugs with coffee. "I'll do it anyway. The old one rattles. Try and eat a bit more breakfast. You're too thin."

Kyle found that Aaron's kindness and that of his friends and his sister Evie took some getting used to. In the few weeks since he left hospital, they seemed to have adopted him, each in their own way. Dave even took him home for the weekend to his house on a cliff where he'd had an amazing time with the German Shepherds he bred, and Evie seemed to delight in buying him new clothes.

The police had interviewed him several times now, and he had his own liaison officer, Alison, who kept him in touch with the legal process. Through her, he knew that Bill had been interviewed, had denied all allegations and had been released. Shocked and frightened, he had talked to Alison who reassured him that investigations were still ongoing, and that Bill's lawyers would stop him from trying anything. Kyle wasn't so sure.

As he quickly tidied up the kitchen, he heard the back door open and he limped along the hall, expecting to see Dave, arriving to collect Stuart for his weekend off.

Dave seemed to be having trouble opening the inner door as his tall shadow dipped and swayed against the glass.

Kyle unlocked the door and pulled it open. "Hi, Dave," he began and almost screamed. As he tried to slam it shut, Spike pushed back, a gleeful smile on his long, narrow face. *How the hell did he find me? Jesus, oh God, please God, No…* His mind garbled as heart thundering, almost peeing in terror, he turned to flee, but was yanked back.

"Don't rush off," Spike said. "Not when I've come all the way to see you."

Helpless, Kyle hung there, almost strangled by the neck of his tee shirt.

"Is your big, handsome nurse in?" Spike asked, shaking him. "Is he a good shag? Hello there, Aaron," he called.

"He's not like that," Kyle choked out.

Spike snorted. "They're all like that."

The straining material around his neck began to rip, and Kyle dropped like a stone, yelling when his legs hit the floor. Coughing and gasping, he grabbed at the wall for support.

"How's the leg?" Spike asked, launching a kick.

Vision blanked white. A scream came from nowhere, and he found himself on his back. Spike stood over him, like the hulking monster he was. "You stupid wee prick," he hissed. "Grassin' to the polis. You know what Bill does to grasses." He looked over his shoulder. "Get your arse in gear, Rodney. Take the wee cunt to the car. I'll have a look around." He ran up the stairs two at a time.

Unable to hold back his wail of pain, Kyle was hauled upright by the scruff of his neck.

The door swung open.

Dave stood in his usual nonchalant stance, a snarling German Shepherd on either side of him.

"Kyle, come over here," Dave said, holding out a hand. "Move one muscle," he said to Rodney, "and the dogs will rip your bastard throat out." He came further into the hall and gripped Kyle's outstretched hand as he hopped towards him.

"Spike's upstairs," Kyle murmured as Dave guided him to lean against the radiator on the nearest wall. At a word from Dave, one of the dogs, pure white and huge, positioned itself beside Kyle.

There was a blur of movement. "Watch out," Kyle yelled. The second dog leapt, grabbed Rodney's arm and forced him to the floor. Dave flung himself into the fray. There was an ear-splitting crack, a howl of pain.

After a second Spike appeared, and in one long movement jumped over the fighting, snarling bodies and ran out the door. "See you soon." His voice echoed.

Chapter Sixteen

The normally quiet, tree-lined street was filled with flashing lights; police uniforms everywhere and neighbours in the road. Then, Aaron saw the ambulance pulling away from outside his own house and he panicked, left the car in the middle of the road and ran to the front door.

A tall policeman blocked his way. "You can't go in there."

"I live here. What's going on?"

"Who are you?" The policeman frowned.

"Aaron Douglas. It's my house. What's happened?"

Before the officer could answer, a man in plain clothes appeared behind him and gestured for the uniformed man to stand aside. "Mr Douglas? I'm Detective Sergeant Salter. Please come through. There's been an incident."

"What kind of incident?" Aaron tried to stay calm. "What's happened? Is someone hurt? Is it Kyle?" The sergeant took his arm in a hard grip and guided him to a series of plastic sheets next to the wall.

"It's a crime scene, sir. Walk here."

Aaron complied, feeling as if he was in the midst of a T.V. drama. "What crime? Why don't you tell me what's going on?"

"It's okay, Sergeant, I'll take it from here." DCI Jones came up the stairs from the kitchen and held out a hand. "Everyone's downstairs, Aaron."

Filled with immediate relief, Aaron complied. "What the hell's going on? Is Kyle alright?"

"Two people broke in to your house and attacked him. It's okay though," she said at Aaron's tense reaction. "He's fine, bit shook up. Dave rescued him."

"Thank fuck." Aaron sighed as he hurried down the stairs behind her. The sight of a woman in white overalls crouching over a patch of blood on the hall floor sent his anxiety sky-high again.

The three figures at the table turned to him with varying expressions of relief and surprise. Stuart, sitting beside a wan-looking Kyle, got up and hugged him.

"Where've you been? I've been trying to phone you."

"Met Evie in town. Somebody tell me what's happened," Aaron said impatiently as he reached the table and Kyle, who grabbed him in a tight hug. Aaron held him, feeling his straining muscles through the thin cotton of his shirt. "Are you okay?" he asked when he could. Kyle nodded against him, not letting go. Aaron's eyes widened at the sight of Dave's blue check shirt covered in blood.

"I'm okay," Dave said. "The guy was shot with his own gun."

Horrified, Aaron looked down at the top of Kyle's head against his chest. "Was it Spike?"

Kyle released his hold and stood back to let Aaron sit down. He nodded, his face a picture of misery. "They know I've spoken to the police. Spike said, 'You know what Bill does to grasses.'" He looked away his slim frame shuddering.

Aaron took in the ripped tee shirt, the drawn face with the wide, shocked looking eyes. "Did he hurt you?" he asked, pulling out the chair beside him. Kyle shook his head and sat, but bruising was visible around his throat. He looked so young and vulnerable that Aaron slid an arm around his shoulders.

"He did hurt him," Dave said. "Beat him up a bit. Kicked his sore leg."

"Bastard," Aaron swore, tightening his arm around Kyle.

"When I arrived, Spike had gone upstairs and his sidekick had a hold of Kyle." Dave continued. "He pulled a gun, and Cooper took him down. Shot himself in the foot, literally."

Aaron looked down in admiration at the two dogs curled asleep beneath the table.

Stuart placed steaming mugs on the table. "Plenty sugar in yours." He smiled at Kyle and turned to Aaron, eyebrows raised. "Cool it, Aro. You look like you're going to explode. We've had time to talk about this. It's time for Kyle to move."

Aaron snorted. "What do you suggest he does? Go back on the streets?"

<>

They argued while Kyle drifted, staring at the skin forming on his cooling chocolate.

Nightmarish memories rose of running and hiding, of huddling with Sean under the motorway flyover and freezing in filthy alleys. Of someone reading a poem at Sean's funeral service and Aaron holding his hand as he wept. His throat ached as he fought back tears and covered his face with his hands. He was vaguely aware of Stuart and Dave leaving, muttering about dogs and gardens. As he struggled to control his emotions, he became aware of Aaron's quiet breathing. The thought of him having to suffer the filthy touch, smell the rancid breath was unthinkable. He knew what he had to do. "I . . . I, have to leave."

"And go where?"

"I don't know, but they'll come back. You're all targets now."

Aaron leaned towards him, his brow creased with concern. "You're not alone anymore," he said, and their heads were so close their breath mingled.

The back door opened. "What the hell's going on here?" asked a woman's voice.

Chapter Seventeen

"Sandi! Why didn't you tell me you were coming today?" Aaron jumped up and moved towards her in the open doorway.

"I did," his wife said, the hurt look on her pretty face, stirring up the usual mixture of guilt and impatience he seemed to feel increasingly in her presence. "I texted you when we landed, but I can see you were busy." As he reached her, she turned away and picked up her rucksack before he could lift it.

"Oh, for God's sake, Sandi," Aaron said, following her and checking his phone which was out of charge.

"And what's going on out there?" She shot over her shoulder as she headed for the stairs. "Police cars everywhere."

The door opened to the two men talking animatedly and the dogs panting and drooling.

"I might have known you'd be here too," Sandi spat at Stuart from halfway upstairs.

"And hello to you too, Sandi," Stuart said and turned to Aaron with eyebrows raised. "Police have finished for the night. They've left a guard. Why didn't you . . . ?" He jerked his head towards Sandi's retreating back.

"I didn't know. Go speak to Kyle, will you? He's for leaving on his own." Aaron edged past the dried blood, which Sandi ignored and followed her upstairs to the bedrooms.

Her slim frame was slumped as she moved along the corridor, dragging her bulging rucksack. Outside their room she flicked back her shoulder length blonde hair, reached for the door handle and hesitated. "Has he been in our bed?" she asked in a small voice.

"No, of course not." As she looked up, he saw that her tear-streaked face was etched with weariness and his annoyance changed to concern. "What is it? Has something happened?"

"Apart from finding my husband snogging his latest boyfriend, you mean?" She flung the door wide as if expecting trouble, but before he could react, she slapped a hand over her mouth and made a dash for the bathroom. When she found the door locked, she emitted a frantic squeal, spun around and vomited into the waste basket.

On an instant, Aaron was there, supporting her and holding her hair back from her mouth as she continued to be sick. When she was done, he lifted her to sit on the bed. He grabbed the box of tissues from her side of the bed and wiped her mouth as she cried. "Hey there, sweetheart," he murmured. "Why didn't you tell me you were ill?"

She sobbed and clutched him closer.

She felt so fragile as he rocked her against him. "You're exhausted. Didn't you sleep at all on the plane?"

"I'm okay." She sighed, pushing herself upright. "Just a bug. Half the squad's down with it." Even with the desert tan, her face was pale and strained looking. She rested against him, letting her head droop on to his shoulder. They breathed together. Her scent rose, reminiscent of happier times, and he kissed her hair. "Why's the bathroom door locked?" she murmured.

"Kyle's using it. He's in the next room."

She jerked away. "I need to sleep."

"Sure." He reached for her jacket.

"I can manage. I just need to sleep."

"Okay. I'll bring you some mint tea to settle your stomach."

"I said, I'm going to sleep." She sat and waited for him to move. After a moment, feeling the sting of rejection, he did.

As he closed the bedroom door, he heard her crying again. His instinct was to return, but knew from the past she was better left alone.

In the living room, Stuart and Dave were arguing. Kyle was sitting on the couch, with the big white dog's head on his lap. All four looked up when he entered.

"What's happening?" Stuart asked.

"I'm sorry I upset your wife," Kyle said.

Aaron shook his head and sat beside him. "Not your fault." He smiled, giving the dog a pat. "She's ill, been sick, and she's sleeping now."

"How long is Sandi staying?" Dave's unexpected question made Aaron blink in surprise. "I know it's her home, but—"

"She's in danger, too, now." Kyle finished. "All because of me."

"It's not all because of you," Aaron said. "It's the fault of the bastards who are trying to hurt you." Kyle turned his head to stroke the dog. Purpling bruises were beginning to show on his neck and the left side of his face, and Aaron felt a rush of protective anger.

"But Sandi being here does raise the stakes," Stuart said.

"Alright, I hear you," Aaron snapped.

"Which brings us to what we were discussing when you were upstairs," Stuart said, ignoring his tone. "When Kyle made his original police statement in the hospital, there was talk of a safe house for him. I think we should follow that up."

"Whereas I think he should come back with me to Port Peter," Dave said.

"Dogs can't stop bullets," Stuart argued.

"Cooper did," Kyle said.

Stuart rolled his eyes.

"You weren't sodding there."

Aaron listened, watching Kyle's colour rise and the defiant look in his eyes. "I take it you want to go with Dave?"

"Yes, and if I can't, I'm leaving anyway."

"Cool it." Aaron smiled. "It's up to you what you do. I'd just be worried that they'd track you down." He looked at Dave. "Your place is a bit remote."

Dave shrugged. "A kennel full of German Shepherds. Me, a friend or two and a couple of veterans who're staying for a few months. The sun and the sea. What more could a young man need?"

"Another young man?" Stuart laughed and bit his lip. "Sorry, Kyle. Wasn't thinking."

Kyle ignored him. "So, that's it, then? I'm coming with you?"

"If that's what you want, son." Dave nodded. "You're very welcome. I can always use another pair of hands to clean up the dog shit."

Kyle looked uncertainly at him, then gave one of his rare smiles.

His face lit up, and his eyes, which seemed to change with his mood, sparkled. The charm and the blaze of it took Aaron's breath away. It was as if the mask slipped, revealing the beauty underneath.

"So, this just leaves the problem of how we're going to get you there without the bastards knowing," Dave said, bringing Aaron back to reality. "Because you can bet your bottom dollar they haven't given up."

"That's what Spike said," Kyle muttered.

<>

Aaron watched in concern as Kyle flattened himself on the floor of the Land Rover, with Meg, the white Shepherd who had adopted him, lying on the seat above. Aaron still hadn't recovered from the nightmare of arriving home to find the place like a page from one of the thrillers he loved to read, and now this seemed like a scene from the *Spooks* TV show Kyle liked.

"He'll be fine, Aro," Stuart said, glancing at him in the half light of the garage. "Dave'll look after him."

Aaron handed over a cushion and blanket for Kyle and some coke and crisps. "I know he will. Just worried you get followed." He felt relieved that the police were taking Kyle's safety so seriously that a young, plain clothes policeman had been assigned to accompany them.

"You're our star witness." The young female DCI had smiled at Kyle when 'The Great Escape' as Stuart called it, had been discussed with her. "We'll liaise with the local station, and they'll keep an eye on you. Alison will let you know how the latest interview with the councillor goes."

"I might dye my hair," Kyle replied. "Be incognito."

Aaron hid a smile, but she took him seriously.

"Good idea, Kyle. Your hair's like a torch."

Aaron watched Dave slam the back door of the vehicle and wink reassuringly, before climbing into the driving seat.

"Try not to worry," Stuart said, clambering in beside Dave. "I'll phone you later."

As the car drove out of the garage, Aaron made a show of waving goodbye to Dave and Stuart as if they were off on their regular trip back home. He waited, watching the car rear lights disappear into the darkness, with no sign of pursuit. Even though he knew an unmarked police car would join them further down the road, he still felt unconvinced of Kyle's safety.

As he turned to go in, a movement to his left caught his eye, and he strode to the dividing wall between his property and his neighbour. He peered into the gnome-infested garden and caught the movement of a larger figure by the fish pond. "Who's there?" he called, tensing for he knew not what. The figure moved, detaching itself from the heron with one-leg-raised which guarded the pond.

"Sorry, it's only me. I was looking for Hercules. He's not in your garage again, is he?"

Aaron drooped with relief. "I'll have a look, Mrs Jackson." He gave an inward groan, recalling the struggle he'd had to grab the cat the last time. As he switched on the garage light, a ball of yowling fluff and claws flew towards him. He leapt backwards as the cat galloped past. "Here he is, Mrs Jackson," he called.

"Where have you been, you naughty boy? Mum's been worried about you."

"I'll try to keep the doors shut in future, Mrs Jackson. Goodnight."

"Is everyone alright, then?" Mrs Jackson's voice was closer. "That carry on was terrible. I said to Dad, that car's up to no good."

Aaron paused and walked towards her as her security light came on. "Did you see the people who broke in?"

"Just the car, son." The old lady stood with the now purring cat in her arms, her head ablaze with multi-coloured hair rollers. "Dad filmed it. It was sat in the street, three days running."

"Did you tell the police?"

"Yes, they took the camera. Dad's not happy." She chuckled, her lined, little smoker's mouth pursed in a conspiratorial smile. "So, is everyone alright? We heard all the noise, dogs barking and somebody yelling. Dad said, 'You'd best phone the police, Elsie.' So, I did, but they were gone before the police got here."

"Did you see them leaving?"

She shrugged and cuddled the cat closer. "Just a glimpse, son. Told the police. Did they get much?"

Chapter Eighteen

After extricating himself from the old lady's conversation, Aaron found Sandi in the living room curled on the sofa in her nightclothes, hands wrapped around a steaming mug. "What's going on?" she asked as soon as he appeared. "Why is there a policeman in the kitchen?"

Aaron sat on an armchair and explained enough of the situation to give her an understanding of what was happening.

She listened with eyes wide, as she sipped from her mug. When he'd finished, she blinked, took a deep breath and exhaled. "So, he's not your boyfriend?"

Aaron held on to his patience. "No, sweetheart, he's just someone I'm trying to help."

"Why the hell didn't you say so then?"

"You didn't give me a chance. As usual, you jumped to the obvious conclusion."

With a lazy smile, she placed her mug on the coffee table and stretched her length on the couch, both hands behind her head. "Is the policeman staying tonight?"

"All night," Aaron said, very aware of her robe falling open and the thrust of her breasts against the thin material of her nightgown. "In case they come back."

"That's not very likely, is it?"

"Hope not," he muttered, as he watched her.

The pale of her slim legs was in contrast to her deeply tanned arms. She stretched again, and he couldn't take his eyes off the toned thighs as the short nightgown slid upwards. He felt himself becoming aroused. Her legs widened, and he glimpsed something odd.

As he leaned forward for a closer look she yanked down the nightgown.

"What's that? he asked.

"What's what?"

"That, on the inside of your thigh. Is it a bruise?"

She waved a dismissive hand. "Just something one of the guys did. Everybody's getting them."

Intrigued, Aaron reached towards her. She pulled away.

"Stop it," she said quickly.

"Hey." He laughed. "You were giving me the come on a minute ago."

"No, I wasn't. I was stretching."

He looked at her with eyebrows raised.

When she impatiently jerked up her gown and spread her legs, his whole body twitched. On the inside of her silken, left thigh in delicate, cursive script was a phrase. He leaned closer. *Every inch a woman, every inch a soldier,* he read, smelling the musk of her. Inhaling, he licked his lips, imagined his tongue tracing upwards to the soft junction between her thigh and groin.

"Paul did that," she said.

Aaron almost gasped aloud. Afraid to speak, lest he growled, afraid to touch lest he lost control, he sat back and crossed his legs.

"He's American, from New York. A combat medic like me. We did training together."

"What else have you done together?"

Her eyes almost popped. He stared, watching for guilt. A flash of something he couldn't catch and she sat up, pulling her clothing around her.

"What the hell do you mean?" she spat, on the attack. "We're not all like you *bi*-sexuals, you know." Her tone was contemptuous "Can't keep it in your—"

"For fuck's sake, Sandi," he exploded. "Pack it in, will you? It happened once, three years ago, and I was pissed. I haven't looked at anyone, man or woman, since." Her eyes were filling up, and he half relented. "I'm sorry, but I've had it. You fling it in my face every time we argue." He looked pointedly at her legs, knees held primly together. "You must have been in a pretty intimate position to get that done. I mean, he must have seen your—"

"Don't be crude." she snapped. "It's a different life out there, I've told you that. We don't have time for the niceties. Paul was a tattooist before he joined up. Likes to keep his hand in."

He bit his lip before blurting something else and looked at her. An attractive face with azure eyes and a full mouth which could twist so sexily as she moaned her climax. They'd known each other since primary school. There were no surprises any longer. He thought she was lying.

"I'm pregnant."

Air puffed from his lungs. "How? When?"

"My last leave of course and as a nurse I'd have thought you'd know how." She winked.

He tried to work out dates. "So, you're about three months? Why didn't you tell me?"

"Didn't want you building up your hopes again until I was sure."

He wanted to believe, so desperately wanted to believe.

"It's twins. Like you and Evie."

That settled it. He grabbed her in a hug and babbled in delight.

"Get off me. You're squeezing too tight." she complained, pushing at him as he playfully kissed her neck.

He let her go, picked up her hands and kissed them. "Thank you, beautiful wife. You're so clever, and I love you."

"Let go, you big, soft lump." She giggled, tugging her hands free.

Overjoyed, he laid a gentle hand over her abdomen and paused in surprise at the soft swelling. "Are you sure it's not triplets? When are you due another scan?"

"There are miscarriage risks with scans in early pregnancy." She slapped his hand away. "They're just big twins. You want healthy babies, don't you? That's why they sent me home early."

He sobered. "Is there a problem? Is that why you were sick?"

She frowned. "It's about avoiding another miscarriage."

Contrite, he pulled a blanket from the back of the sofa and began to tuck it around her. She yawned and half-heartedly slapped at his arms. "Don't fuss, Aaron. I'm fine. Just a bit tired from the flight and the bug. I'm going back to bed."

<>

She lay there pretending to sleep, watching through lowered eyelids, as he tiptoed around the room unpacking her clothes and putting them away. *Leave it,* she wanted to scream. He was so fussy, always tidying, cleaning. Wouldn't last ten minutes in Afghan. She stopped, shocked at her thoughts. She loved him, had always loved him, still loved him, didn't she? He began to undress, pulling off his tee shirt and unbuckling his jeans. She had to admit, for a civilian, he kept himself fit. Wide shoulders and narrow waist, muscles toned and sleek as he headed for the shower.

For a moment she allowed herself to remember that other body, powerful, hairy, with big, gentle hands. He was also a twin, but there the comparison stopped. Paul adored her with a passion Aaron could never match, arousing her to heights she had never known existed. A sob escaped, and she ducked under the duvet and began the litany. *It was just a fling. He's dead.* A technicolour memory swamped her mind. The Lynx air support swooping out of the sky like an avenging angel, door gunners scattering the surrounding enemy. Amid the scramble of the few remaining squad clambering aboard, he had lifted her, thrown her upwards to be grabbed by the crew. She had fought to the open doorway, desperately reaching out. Their eyes had locked. His olive skin shone in the ferocious sunlight before, under machine gun fire, the helicopter swept away. They had returned and searched, but of Paul, no sign.

<>

Aaron knew that the days of crawling into bed with her, naked and excited, were long gone. Their most recent sex had been ruled by temperatures and times in an effort to get pregnant, and even then, she'd always insisted that he pull on pyjama pants the moment after he climaxed. Although he'd done so to keep the peace, he'd resented it, and still did, as he yanked on his pants after his shower.

As he tiptoed to his side of the bed, he heard her sobbing as if her heart was broken. Without a word, he lay down, curled around her protectively and held her close. When the storm had passed, and she slept in his arms, he lay awake, gazed into the darkness and remembered their past.

She'd been a lifesaver, helping him to pick up the pieces after Stuart had left, when all he wanted to do was curl into a ball and howl. He'd sunk into despair, smoking weed and having repetitive drink-fuelled, anonymous sex. Then, one day, Sandi had appeared. She cleaned him up and encouraged him to continue with his nursing degree, showering him with a lifetime of accumulated love. For her, marriage to him was the pinnacle of success. For him, although he cared and tried to be the husband she seemed to want, he'd always felt like a disappointment, and that something was missing in the relationship. He believed her when she said it was a child, so they tried for a baby, but two miscarriages later, they began to drift apart. When she joined the Army Medical Corps two years into their marriage, he felt it was a relief for them both. A year later and she was again desperate to have a child. He'd gone along with it, although home leave became complicated, but this time they seemed to have succeeded.

She sighed, cuddled against him and muttered in her sleep. A vision of the tattoo filled his mind, and a wave of jealousy took him by surprise. It had never occurred to him before that she might be unfaithful, but the touch of that too-rounded belly beneath his hand raised questions. Confused and frustrated, he spiralled into restless sleep.

Chapter Nineteen

Kyle awoke to sunshine in his eyes. His room was bathed in golden light, and he could hear distant barking interspersed with the regular crunching whump of blade hitting log. Uncertain of the time but sure he should have been up, he got out of bed, threw the curtains aside and gazed out at the view. His previous experience of the seaside was as a young child in foster care and involved memories of sand in sandwiches he didn't want and a foster mum yelling at him for getting his clothes wet. This time, he was loving every minute.

Although the sea was quite a distance from Dave's clifftop eyrie, he recognised the two kennel volunteers playing football on the beach with four barking dogs. Axe in hand and looking up at the window, Dave was standing in the garden, a pile of split logs beside him. Kyle opened the window.

"Bout time you were up," Dave called. "Your breakfast was almost in a dog."

"Okay, thanks," Kyle yelled back.

He felt so energised in the shower that he jerked off. Occasionally, some of the men who'd used him had thought that masturbating him somehow made everything alright. Usually, he hadn't become aroused, which made them angry, or he'd had an unwilling orgasm, which left him feeling empty and ashamed. His cock hardly ever got hard anymore, and sometimes he'd thought it had died, but standing in Dave's bath with the old-fashioned shower sputtering above him, he revelled in his own sexuality. He threw back his head and yelled his release to the accompaniment of the groaning plumbing.

In the kitchen, he made sandwiches of crispy bacon and leathery eggs and enjoyed every morsel with a huge mug of builder's tea. He took a mug out to Dave, who nodded in gratitude, sweat running in rivulets down his tanned face and into his beard.

Dave sat on one of the ornate looking benches, hand-carved by Stuart, gulped his tea and smacked his lips. "That's good, son. You're official tea-maker from now on."

Kyle grinned and sat on a chair shaped like a seated man, effectively sitting in the man's lap. He didn't know why, but he couldn't get his head around the idea of graceful Stuart sawing wood.

"How did you sleep?"

"Okay," Kyle muttered, turning to look out to sea. On the far horizon he could just make out the shape of an oil rig flickering in the heat haze.

"I heard you shouting."

"I'm sorry." Kyle shrugged, embarrassed.

"I'm not complaining, son," Dave said quietly. "When I was in the Forces, I had nightmares all the time." He nodded when Kyle looked around in surprise. "Most of us did. I had my share, too, before I left the police." He sat there, eyes narrowed against the sun, the epitome of tough manhood.

"I . . . I didn't know. I thought it was just me."

"No way." Dave grinned in the wolfish way he had, like one of his dogs. "I think you might also have flashbacks? Like waking nightmares?"

Kyle could only stare at him, astonished.

"Thought so. It's called PTSD, which means post-traumatic stress disorder." Dave smiled. "Don't look so worried, son. You can get over it."

Kyle felt his throat tighten like he wanted to cry. It wasn't his fault. Other people felt like this too. He became aware that Dave had moved to crouch beside him.

"Kyle, listen to me. You're not in control of this. You can't help it." Hearing the calm, deliberate words, Kyle took a deep breath and shakily exhaled. Dave patted him on the shoulder. "Good boy," he said.

In spite of himself, Kyle smiled. "I'm not a dog."

Dave leaned back on his knees. "Stuart says that too sometimes."

Kyle looked into the compassionate blue eyes and knew that he could trust this man. "How did you get through it then?"

"It wasn't easy. Took a hell of a lot of hard work. Have you thought of counselling or therapy?"

Kyle shrugged, picturing lying on a couch speaking to someone in a chair. He didn't like the idea of that at all.

Dave moved back to the bench. "I know a place, not far from here, that specialises in helping people through trauma. It's called Crannog, which means 'a safe place'. They do counselling, but they also have a gym, swimming pool and alternative therapies like massage. They do walking groups and barbeques on the beach, and they have dogs."

Kyle was impressed. "Did you go there?"

Dave nodded. "A few years ago now. Best thing I ever did." He grinned and raised one eyebrow. "Apart from marrying Stuart."

Kyle smiled.

"I want to tell you something else," Dave said in a serious tone. "After I joined the army when I was sixteen, my mum remarried. My sister Helen was twelve. Our stepfather raped Helen for two years before it all came out. She was pregnant, lost the baby and hanged herself."

Kyle felt an icy coldness in the pit of his stomach. His mouth was dry. "God . . . I'm so sorry," he managed to get out.

"You're stronger than she was," Dave said. "You're a veteran who's been to hell and back and you're still fighting."

Ashamed, Kyle shook his head. "I've thought about killing myself," he whispered. "Cut myself when I was younger. In school, we'd pass blades around, dare each other to do it. Some guys even cut their wrists. Two died." He swallowed hard to keep his breakfast down. "People think when they – you know – it's just like two men having sex, but it's not . . . I don't think." He finished in an uncertain tone and looked down at the sandy soil.

"No, it's not." Dave leaned towards him. "What happened to you was abuse, plain and simple. Something precious that should have been yours to give and share was stolen from you," he said, voice firm and true. "You're strong and brave, Kyle, and with the right help, you will recover from this. It might not feel like it now, but you will."

Kyle raised his head and took in Dave's steady, determined gaze.

"Paedophiles come from all walks of life." Dave said. "My last few years with the police were with a Sexual Offences team." he continued, leaning back in his chair. "We rescued several young people and prosecuted a few traffickers. The youngsters got a lot of help, but . . . " He rolled his eyes. "Often the bastards either got off due to lack of evidence or disappeared into the woodwork."

"Do you think that's what he'll do? Get off and disappear into the woodwork?" Kyle asked, his stomach churning at the thought of Bill coming after him. A picture raced across his mind of a spider scuttling through a crack in a floorboard. He shuddered.

Dave shook his head. "You met Max, my old DI? She just doesn't give up. What her team is focussing on is gathering as much evidence from witnesses as possible, so he can't talk his way out of it when it gets to court." Dave paused. "What you need to do is get better so you can cope with testifying against him in court."

Kyle stared at him, taking in the scary reality of what he was saying. "And . . . and this place could help me to get better?"

"Yup," Dave said, getting to his feet. "Lot to think about, son. I need to check on the breeding bitches. We can talk later."

Chapter Twenty

Kyle spent the morning thinking through Dave's words while doing housework tasks he had little experience of. He had taken his turn at washing dishes and tidying up in Aaron's house, but a cleaner did the major tasks. The washing machine was a mystery, which he only solved by studying the instruction booklet. The vacuum cleaner was easier, but an inch closer and he'd have lost a foot trying to chop wood with the huge axe. He gave up and sliced bread to be eaten with Dave's homemade chicken soup for lunch.

"Pity you can't walk the dogs with us," said Nick, the young volunteer whose smiles and looks made Kyle feel uncomfortable.

"The boot won't work on the sand." Kyle kept his gaze firmly on Nick's bowl as he ladled in more soup. "And I can't get down the path," he added, turning away when Nick opened his mouth to reply.

"Anymore bread?" asked Charlie, the other one.

"Get it yourself, Chaz," Dave chided. "He's not your servant."

"It's ok," Kyle said, limping over to the kitchen unit. "There's plenty here." He refilled the bread basket and returned with it to the table. As he sat back down to finish his own lunch, he was aware of Nick's gaze. He knew that, like Charlie, Nick was a veteran of Afghanistan, but unlike Charlie who didn't seem to have a mark on him, Nick had a scar from his right temple which ran to his neck, disappearing under his clothes. With his shoulder length, blond hair, he looked like a Viking warrior from the sagas Kyle had watched in Aaron's flat.

"So, what are the plans for this afternoon?" Dave asked, interrupting his thoughts. "I'm going into the village, if anyone needs anything."

"Cigarettes, m-mate," Charlie said stretching long arms above his shining, bald head, "and it's k-kennel c-cleaning for me."

"And me," said Nick. "What about you, Kyle? D'you want to help?"

Thinking the last thing he wanted to do was clean up shit, Kyle nodded and began to gather dishes together.

"No, leave them Kyle," Dave said. "You go off and enjoy yourself." He grinned.

The kennel was a large, purpose-built structure, looking from the outside like a barn. Within, it had heating, air conditioning and individual areas for dogs at various stages of their training and development. There were eight large, powerful looking German Shepherds of various colours, four studs and four bitches, who each had an individual run and comfortable sleeping area. Next to them were four younger dogs who were in training for the army and in a separate section, one heavily pregnant female lay panting on her side. Two other females, each with pups, seemed to Kyle, to be watching her in concern.

"D-Danka's started early." Charlie stammered more when stressed. "N-Nick, g-go and see if D-Dave's left yet. She'll need the v-vet soon."

When Nick left, Kyle crouched beside Danka and gently stroked her head. She was a beautiful dog, whose shining coat was the colour of a fox. Her huge, doggy eyes looked up at him with what he thought was desperation, and he whispered to her and lightly laid his fingers on her swollen, straining stomach where he was sure he could feel movement. He slid her water dish closer to her.

"She won't drink, Kyle," Dave said from behind him, "but you could wet her lips from the water bowl. The vet's on her way."

For Kyle, the birth was the most incredible experience of his life and one he knew he'd never forget. Danka's first pup had become jammed in the birth canal, and he watched from the floor beside Nick as the young, female vet manoeuvred its dead little body free and handed it to Dave to wrap in a towel. On the edge of tears, Kyle watched as one by one, the little pup's siblings were born. At the sight of the tiny creatures blindly seeking their mother, he half cried and half laughed. Beside him, Nick seemed to be in a similar state, and when his arm slid around Kyle's shoulders, it felt like a gesture of camaraderie.

Later, they prepared a meal together, finally settling on bacon and scrambled eggs when they couldn't think of anything else they could cook. They talked easily, and Kyle found himself enjoying listening to Nick's Newcastle accent as he talked about how he came to be volunteering with Dave for the summer.

"I'd left the AA meeting before it began properly and straight into the pub. I was on my third whisky when I saw this guy come in," Nick said as he beat the eggs in a bowl. "He stood there at the door, like he was looking for somebody, then he headed straight for me, even knew my name. He told me about when he was at his lowest, in the gutter he called it, then it was like that Bible story, you know? The one where Jesus tells them to follow him and be fishermen or something. So I did. Never had a drink from that day to this." Nick chuckled and reached across Kyle for the pan and wooden spoon.

Kyle reached it first and turned to hand it to him. The man was close, an unmistakable expression in his blue eyes which made Kyle's belly twist in fear. He froze. Nick raised his hand and gently stroked his knuckle down Kyle's cheek.

Kyle flinched back, almost staggering into the table. "What're you doing?" he yelled. "What do you think I am?"

"I'm sorry. God, I'm sorry," Nick garbled. "I made a mistake. I thought you were—"

"What? You thought I was what?"

"Gay," Nick said, eyes troubled. "I'm sorry, Kyle. I just thought you were the same as me. I . . . I didn't mean anything. I'm so sorry."

Confused and embarrassed, Kyle turned to go. Dave was standing in the open doorway. "What's going on?" He frowned.

"It doesn't matter," Kyle said, squeezing past him and going to his room. He took off his support boot and lay on his bed. His leg throbbed. The word 'gay' rattled around in his head. He knew what it was supposed to mean, although was never sure if being shagged by men made you that way. He'd seen some of the boys in school kissing and doing it to each other in the showers. On the other hand, Terry had a girlfriend, and Jason always used to make comments about women's bodies on TV. Sean was definitely gay, but Dave and Stuart just seemed like ordinary guys. And now there was Nick, with his magnetic eyes, scarred face and gentle touch.

There was a knock on the door. "Kyle, it's Dave. Can I come in?"

After a reluctant few seconds, Kyle answered in the affirmative.

Dave's friendly, concerned face appeared. "How's it going, son?" he asked, closing the door behind him. "Did Nick say something to offend you?"

"No," Kyle said. "It's not him, it's me. I need to sort myself out." Dave sat on the edge of the bed and raised one eyebrow. "Nick said he thought I was gay."

"And do you think you are?"

Kyle shrugged and fiddled with the bedcover. "I was fucked enough, so I must be," he whispered.

"Nobody can make you gay, or straight," Dave said in a matter-of-fact tone. "It's how you're born."

It was a revelation. Kyle looked up into the warm gaze. "Are you sure?"

"Absolutely." Dave nodded. "I knew when I was six years old. I tried to kiss my best mate. He walloped me with a toy bus." He grinned. "I never tried that again, at least not with him. Stuart knew even earlier."

Kyle gazed into the distance and tried to think back to his own childhood memories, but everything was confused. "My mum died when I was six," he said. "Can't remember much after that. Was in foster care for a while, then, then the school. I don't remember trying to kiss anyone – ever." He smiled to cover embarrassment. Dave was silent and seemed to be looking at him with drawn brows. "What . . . what's up?"

"Nothing, sorry." Dave quickly shook his head. "I was just thinking how much the Centre will help you. If you want, we could go for a visit."

"Okay, where is it?"

"On an island, about two hours from here, but before you decide anything, come into the village with me later. There's someone I want you to meet."

Chapter Twenty-one

As Dave powered along the motorway to Glasgow, his thoughts were with the brave, young man he had waved goodbye to at the quay. Kyle had looked nervous but resolute as he'd waved back from Owen's truck, with the dog crates strapped in the back. "Don't let this old reprobate lead you astray, Kyle," Dave had said half seriously. "If he mentions going to the pub, run like hell."

"Och, don't listen to him, Kyle son. Maybe just a wee dram." Owen had winked, and Kyle had grinned in reply.

Dave was relieved that they had hit it off. He knew that his old army friend could be an awkward customer, but Owen had surprised him by taking to Kyle immediately and treating him with the instinctive kindness he'd seen him employ in the past with scared, young recruits. There was a solidity and sense of safety around Owen, to which nervous creatures, including the dogs he trained, responded.

He pulled into a pub car park frequented by off-duty police and checked his mobile for messages. A text from Stuart confirming their meeting in a bar with Aaron when they'd finished work, and another from Nick, saying that the dog food order had arrived.

It wasn't a secret meeting; he was, after all, having a drink with his old DI, but they still huddled in a corner and kept their voices low. Laughter and jokes swirled around them, and occasionally Dave found himself caught in the ritual of handshaking and back-slapping with old mates.

"So, tell me about this councillor?" Dave asked, as he tried to blend in with the walls plastered with old yellowed notices advertising club-nights and charity events.

Max took a sip of her coke. The daughter of alcoholic parents, she never touched the stuff. "He's married, childless and a local councillor with ambitions to become an M.P. Promotes himself as a 'man of the people.' Does lots of charity work, etc." She rolled her eyes. "He's been of interest to Operation Undertow for some time. Production and distribution of child porn, and we're sure he's a major player in a European-wide paedophile and people trafficking network. Nothing's ever stuck, so far, and he walks out laughing."

"And now?"

Max shrugged. "We got some useful info from Rodney Grey, the guy you and your dog caught, then, all of a sudden, a solicitor appeared and he stopped talking."

"Isn't legal aid wonderful?" Dave snorted, taking a mouthful of tonic water.

Max leaned closer. "The fiscal says there's insufficient evidence so far, but as well as Kyle, we have three other boys prepared to testify to their treatment in the residential school, and we're trying to find teachers who've left." She emptied the remains of her coke into a glass. "Did you know Kyle also worked in the councillor's office as an admin worker?"

Dave blinked in surprise.

"It makes him key to the investigation and his safety is paramount. Is he still with you?"

Dave nodded and filled her in about the island therapy centre. "If he likes it, and they think he's suitable; if they have a vacancy, and if we can find the money to fund it, he'll move soon."

She raised her dark eyebrows. "That's a lot of ifs."

"It's not a charity." Dave shrugged. "But they do great work with PTSD."

Her eyes narrowed. "Was that where . . . ?"

"Yes, they got me back on the straight and narrow after Iraq."

"Well, keep me in the loop and that boy safe. The councillor is a dangerous man." She finished her drink and nodded at Dave's half empty glass.

"No, thanks, I'm meeting Stuart and Aaron later."

<>

Although aware that Stuart would object, Dave took a detour to make a couple of under-the-counter purchases which he locked in the boot of his Land Rover. He spotted Stuart as soon as he entered the half-empty bar, hunched over a table against the wall, engaged in what looked to be a serious conversation with Aaron.

"Am I interrupting?" He smiled, kissing Stuart and squeezing Aaron's shoulder before he sat down.

Stuart looked at Aaron with one eyebrow raised until Aaron nodded.

"Aaron's doubting the babies are his," Stuart said, without preamble. "He thinks Sandi's had an affair."

"In Afghanistan?" Dave queried.

Aaron nodded.

"But how? I mean how can you be sure?"

"I'm not, I'm just suspicious. Some things like dates just don't add up."

"But they're twins, aren't they?"

"Lots of people are." Aaron's smile was wry, and he shrugged as if dismissing the subject and signalled the waiter. "D'you want a drink? Same again, Stu?"

Once they'd settled down again, Dave filled them in on his meeting with Max.

"More witnesses, takes the pressure off Kyle, surely?" Stuart suggested. "And more evidence means the bastard will definitely go down."

"I suppose it should, but he's a slippery customer with a crooked legal team."

"So, what's Max's advice?"

"To take all precautions to keep Kyle safe. He's a key witness."

"Is he alright?" Aaron entered the conversation, eyes lit with concern.

"He's fine. In fact, he's more than fine." Dave smiled. "He sleeps till lunchtime, eats like a horse and I swear he's grown two inches." He was pleased when Aaron grinned in response. "I've been talking to him about getting some help with his PTSD," he went on, explaining about the island therapeutic centre. "In fact, he's over there now for a visit with a mate of mine. If it's suitable, they'll book him in for a week's assessment and if he's offered a place, we just need to find the funding."

"I'll pay," Aaron said at once.

"Careful, Aro," Stuart said softly, "I know you're committed to helping him, but—"

"I said I'll pay," Aaron said to Dave. "Whatever it takes to get him healed and keep him safe."

"What about Sandi?" Stuart asked.

Aaron shook his head. "Nothing to do with her."

Chapter Twenty-two

"What d'you mean he's not there now?" Bill roared, leaning across his desk.

Spike took a careful sidestep to avoid the spray of saliva. Beside him, Gary, who wasn't as quick, caught the full impact.

"There's just no sign of him, boss." Gary surreptitiously wiped his face.

"I thought you said he was there, Spike?" Bill spluttered.

"He was. I nearly had him if it hadn't been for the dogs." Despite his long association with the man, Spike tensed as Bill pinned him with a malevolent stare.

"Dogs," Bill sneered. "What have you got a gun for?" He shifted his gaze to Gary who was beginning to tremble. "So who is living there?"

"Two gay guys." Gary flinched as Bill's fist thumped the desk.

"Bet they've had some fun, for nothing." He glared at Gary. "So, why didn't you grab one of them?"

"They've got protection, Bill, a cop on the door." Gary's tone became ingratiating. "I left a calling card."

Bill ignored him and flung himself back into his executive chair. He began to rock back and forth, the silence broken by creaking. "We have to find the little shite," he finally hissed. "What I did for that boy. Took him out the muck. Gave him a top job. And what does he do? First chance he gets, he goes running to the pigs." He sadly shook his head. "They've no gratitude these days."

Spike nodded in commiseration. "What do you want Gary to do, Bill?"

Eyes bright, Bill sat up straight. "Find him." His gaze shifted to Gary. "Text me the address, and I'll take care of the copper. You grab one of these gay guys and make him tell you where the wee grass is. By whatever means necessary. Am I making myself clear?" Gary nodded. Bill dismissed him with a wave of his hand, a diamond sparkling on his wedding finger.

Spike stood uncertainly for a moment and turned to leave.

"Hang on, Spike. Sit down a minute."

Spike sat in the chair before the desk, hiding his relief when Bill produced a bottle of whisky and two glasses.

"Thing is, Spike," Bill said, pouring each of them a dram. "I need to go away for a bit and I want you to sort out a few things for me."

"You're going away?" Spike said in surprise, knocking his drink back in one.

Bill nodded and took a sip of his own. "Police are getting too close. My lawyers are advising that I lay low for a bit, so I'm going into a clinic for a rest due to overwork." He slowly winked, making Spike smile in response. "You can visit me every week to keep me in the loop and I'll be on the end of the phone if you need me."

"Okay, boss. What do you want me to do?"

With a sigh Bill leaned back, clasped his hands across his round belly and began to issue instructions. "The European shipments are too slow. Contact Alina, find out what the hold-up is and fix it. If she's the problem, get rid of her and find somebody else to take over. If it's a borders or customs problem, pay them off. I've got customers waiting and they won't wait forever."

Chapter Twenty-three

The powerful headlights illuminated the drive, highlighting the flaking blue paint of the garage doors. As he climbed out of the car, Aaron felt relieved and somewhat surprised that Stuart had remembered to close the doors when he left for work earlier. Driving inside, his eyes widened at a scene straight out of a horror movie. He stared, unable to believe what he was seeing. Bulging eyes, matted hair and blood. Confused, he jumped out and switched on the garage light. The cat hung crucified against the back wall. He rushed to it, but mercifully, the small sharp teeth were bared rigidly in death. Before he could fully take it in, a greater terror filled his mind.

"Sandi." He leapt back and ran for the front door. No policeman stood guard at the open door. Praying he was inside having a cuppa, Aaron skidded along the wooden floor of the hall, knocking aside the coat stand. In pyjamas and dressing gown, Sandi stood filling the kettle at the sink. She turned at his sudden entrance.

"Where's your policeman?" Aaron said without preamble.

"He was called away."

"When?"

"An hour or so ago, why? What's wrong Aaron? You're white as a sheet."

"Is there anyone else in the house?"

"No, why?"

"The front door was open."

Sandi looked surprised. "Was it? I didn't know—"

"Stay here." Aaron cut her off. "Keep this door closed, and if you hear anything, scream."

"Hear what?" she said as he ran out of the room.

Grabbing Kyle's discarded walking stick from the hall stand, Aaron explored the house, but nothing seemed out of place. With the picture of the poor cat in his mind, he ran around locking doors and windows. Back in the kitchen, he took Sandi's hand and led her protesting upstairs.

"Get some clothes on and pack a case. You're going to Evie's."

"I don't want to go to Evie's."

Aaron caught her by the shoulders, feeling her fragility through the thinness of her gown. "Please, sweetheart. Just the once, don't argue, do as I ask."

Sandi looked up at him with a puzzled expression. "Has something happened?"

"I'll tell you later. Please hurry." Kissing her brow, he turned and galloped downstairs again. Back outside, he reversed the car onto the road, locked the garage doors, phoned his sister and the police. The street seemed normal, with only familiar cars parked outside houses, but he checked again to make sure before he brought Sandi down and settled her in the car.

She was annoyed and showed it as she yanked the seatbelt around herself. "You'd better have a good reason for all this," she said. He told her what had happened and her mouth dropped open. "That's horrible. Why would anyone do that? Shouldn't we phone the police?"

"I have done. Just wanted to get you safe first."

When she was silent, he glanced around and caught the warmest expression he'd seen for a long time, reflected in passing headlights.

As always, Aaron felt that mixture of confusion and guilt as he sped up on the motorway heading for his sister's home.

In a fitted, black dress and high heels Evie rushed out to the car and flung her arms around Sandi.

"You going out?" Aaron asked.

"Not now," Evie replied. "And don't say a word, Sandi. It's just one of Cameron's boring dinners anyway. I'd much rather spend time with you."

Aaron leaned down and kissed her cheek as he passed with Sandi's bag. "Thank, sis."

"No problem." She smiled, turning her elfin face up to return the kiss. "Just take it to the spare room. Are you staying for a cuppa?"

"No time, sis. I've got to get back to the flat before Stuart does." With Evie yelling at him to be careful, he got back in the car and drove off.

He knew he hadn't made it when he saw the police vehicles in the street outside the house and the open garage doors. In a panic, he rushed to the house, but before he could give his name to the police officer at the door, Stuart bounded out and flung his arms around him.

In utter relief, Aaron hugged him back.

"Thank God, oh thank God. I got your text but when you weren't here thought they'd grabbed you again," Stuart gasped against his neck. "Are you okay?" His eyes raked Aaron's face.

"I'm fine. I took Sandi to Evie's."

"That monstrosity in the garage." Stuart's full lips curled in disgust. "What kind of swine would do that to a defenceless animal? Is Sandi alright?"

"She's fine. Are you okay?"

"Sorry to interrupt," said a voice.

Aaron turned to the serious looking dark-haired woman.

"Glad you're safe, Aaron. DCI Maxine Jones, Dave's friend?"

"Of course." Aaron shook her hand in relief. "Glad you're on the case."

A woman in a baggy, white suit squeezed passed them with a muttered apology.

"Let's go sit in the car," Max said.

Aaron watched another similarly dressed figure with a camera, walking from the garage to the house. "What's going on?"

"The back door's been forced. Your kitchen and study have been ransacked."

Shocked, Aaron stared at her. "When? I mean, I was only away a couple of hours."

"When did you leave?"

"About eight."

"And I got home about ten," Stuart said. "What were they looking for?"

Max shrugged. "Apart from the poor cat, did you notice anything unusual?" She asked Aaron.

Aaron thought back and shook his head. "After I found the cat, I checked the house. Sandi was in the kitchen." He shrugged. "No sign of a break-in then. Now I wish I'd phoned you lot before I left, but I was terrified for her safety. She's pregnant. I didn't check next door either. It's their cat, but they haven't been around for a few days. I've been feeding it."

She nodded understanding. "Was there a police officer on the door?"

"No. Sandi said he'd been called away." He watched Max's brows crease in a frown as she got out the car to use her mobile. "What happened when you got here?" he asked Stuart.

"Saw the thing in the garage just as the police arrived, then, I phoned Dave. Everything's fine down there."

"What the hell's happening, Stu?" Aaron muttered, watching the activity through the window. "It's like we've slid into a different dimension."

"It's certainly a scary world young Kyle escaped from," Stuart said. "And this is a crime scene now. We can't stay."

Aaron thought of the two options, camp at the hospital or camp at Evie's. Neither was appealing.

"We're both on days off. Why don't we go down to the Port?" Stuart suggested.

An immediate flash of pleasure at the thought of sea, sand and seeing Kyle, was quickly squashed by guilt and a sense of duty. "Sandi." Aaron sighed. "I can't leave her and she won't want to come."

"You think her and Evie will want you there getting in the way of all the baby shopping?" Stuart said from the darkness. "Come on, Aro, we need a break and Dave says Kyle's backing off going to the island now. He needs help."

Aaron's sense of duty warred with his driving need to protect Kyle. "I'll go back to Evie's tonight and talk to Sandi. Drive down tomorrow." He felt rather than saw Stuart's smile as Max climbed back into the front seat.

She slid around to face them. "There's been a development."

Chapter Twenty-four

Stuart plonked two cans of lager on the rough-hewn table next to a battered-looking walkie-talkie and sat down beside Aaron. "Never got around to finishing this," he said, running his fingers over the table top.

"Yeah, still a bit lumpy, mate." Aaron pulled the tab and took a sip of the cold liquid with an appreciative murmur.

"Glad we came?"

"Uh-huh."

Dave swore loudly from the woodshed where he was chopping up logs.

"He's obsessed," Stuart said, "I think it's some form of OCD. Either that, or he's redirecting his sexual energy."

Aaron raised cynical eyebrows, and Stuart grinned as Dave came out from the shed.

"See what I found, sweetheart," Dave said in an innocent voice. In his hand, gripped between thumb and forefinger was the biggest insect Aaron had ever seen.

With a leap which overturned his chair, Stuart was behind Aaron. "Don't you dare, Davie."

"D'you think he's going to protect you?" Dave grinned, slowly walking closer, the creature wriggling in his grasp.

Aware of Stuart's phobia, Aaron stood too, ready for he knew not what.

"I'm warning you, Davie. Bring that near me and, and . . . " Stuart's voice held a note of panic.

"Leave it, Dave," Aaron said.

With a roll of his eyes and a chuckle, Dave halted. "What a pair of wimps you two are. It's only a wee spider, disturbed from its cosy nest."

"Throw it back in its cosy nest then," Stuart said, holding tight to the back of Aaron's tee-shirt. Aaron nodded in agreement.

With a disbelieving shake of his head, Dave returned the creature to the shed and came over to Stuart. "Cool it, babe," he said, hugging him and kissing his neck. "I won't do that again, I promise."

"You'd better not."

"Or what?" Dave smiled, winking at Aaron. "What'll you do to me?"

"It's what I won't do that you should be bothered about."

Dave murmured something which made Stuart softly laugh, and Aaron turned away. For a moment he felt a jealousy, easily dismissed. He knew they adored each other and could not begrudge them their happiness, but he yearned for just a moment of such loving intimacy. A movement on the table caught his eye.

The walkie-talkie lying next to a screwdriver, as if awaiting repair, was making clicking noises and shuffling back and forth.

"This thing's alive," he said.

"Help, Dave, help," the machine squawked.

"What the hell?" Stuart said, exchanging a startled look with Aaron as Dave rushed through the open kitchen door, and seconds later, emerged holding a gun.

"Come on," he yelled to them, as Stuart squeaked in shock. "They're being attacked."

"What's going on?" gasped Aaron, half out of his chair.

"Kyle," Dave shouted as he ran for the path down the cliff. "They're after Kyle."

Heart leaping in his chest, Aaron pounded after him, almost tumbling over the edge. Stuart grabbed him and propelled him in the right direction. Eyes straining, Aaron could just make out the two fleeing figures, trailed by two dogs. On their tail, two other figures made heavy weather of ploughing through the sand. As they drew closer, he saw that the leading figure was carrying someone over his shoulder, someone who was struggling and whose hair blazed in the sunshine.

Dave reached the beach first. He continued running, calling the dogs to him as he raced towards the pursuers. Aaron was next, coming to a halt as the tall, bald man reached him and tumbled Kyle into his arms, before turning to follow Dave. Kyle fought on, swearing at the top of his voice.

"Cool it, Kyle. You're safe now," Aaron gasped, struggling to hold his lithe, wriggling body. He was aware of Stuart running past as a man he'd been introduced to as Nick, caught up and reached his hand towards Kyle, who brushed it off.

"Get off. Let me go," Kyle panted.

"You're ok. You're safe," Aaron said, hugging him against his chest with both arms.

"I'll fucking kill them," Kyle yelled, making Aaron change his assessment.

"He wants to punch their lights out," Nick said in admiration. With effort, Aaron spun Kyle around so that he could hold him by the shoulders. Kyle stilled and glared at him.

"Cool it." Aaron said quietly.

Kyle's gaze was mutinous, his lips drawn in a stubborn line. His normally pale skin looked tanned and healthy, with a light dusting of freckles across his nose and cheeks. "Fucking kill them," he repeated.

"Calm down."

The fight seemed to go out of Kyle. His face crumpled. "How do they always know where I am?" He wailed, surprising Aaron by hugging him. "I've missed you."

A gunshot rang out.

They jerked as one and turned to the shore. "They're on the run," Kyle exclaimed, bouncing with excitement.

Aaron kept a hold of him in case he decided to bounce after them. He watched with a mixture of relief and growing anger as the pursuers became the pursued. Within seconds it was all over. Brought down by the dogs, the two men were grabbed by Dave, and the tall, bald man, searched and marched along the beach. "That dog bit me." Aaron heard one of the prisoners complain as they came closer.

"His teeth are cleaner than yours." Dave snarled.

Aaron became aware of a terrible anger taking root within him as they stumbled along in their pseudo-leather jackets and jeans, city shoes sinking in the sand. Faced with the minions of an evil beyond his ken, he wanted to shield and protect the slim, young man by his side.

As they came abreast, the nearest one spat at Kyle and before Aaron could react, Kyle swung a punch which connected sharply with the man's nose. Blood spurted, the man's howl drowned by Stuart's congratulatory shout.

"He broke ma fuckin' dose," the man yelped, as Kyle danced around hissing and shaking his hand in the air. Nick again reached for him, but was impatiently shrugged off.

"S . . . serves you f . . . fuckin' right," the bald man said, hauling him on.

Speechless with astonishment, Aaron took Kyle's hand in his own and gently examined it. He looked into the pain-filled grey eyes. "Nothing broken. What's happened to you?"

"I'm sticking up for myself," Kyle said, half laughing, half crying as he cradled his sore hand. "And I can walk without my boot, most of the time."

Aaron grinned with affection and pride. "Well done," he said and watched Kyle blush at the praise.

"Hey, nice one, slugger." Stuart chuckled, patting Kyle's shoulder as he jogged past after Dave.

PART TWO

Chapter Twenty-five

"Sorry," the girl said.

It was the second time she had bumped into him, and Kyle was beginning to think it was deliberate. Hauling his bulging rucksack further up his back, he continued to watch the waving figures as the land receded. The race to catch the ferry had been stressful but great fun, especially when Stuart had almost fallen out of the speedboat, and Dave and Aaron had to drag him back. Kyle could see him now, waving enthusiastically, so he must have recovered. Restraining a childish need to blow kisses, he waved back hard and scrabbled in his pocket for his phone. It was one of Aaron's leaving gifts, and he hadn't got the hang of using it yet. By the time it was ready to take a picture, the figures on land had lost clarity. His throat tightened, and he swallowed hard. Another jerk on his rucksack and he turned in annoyance.

She was a study in black; hair, eyes and clothes.

"Watch it," he muttered, and returned to his vigil. The three figures were moving away. He was sure it was Aaron who turned around and raised a hand in a last farewell. Reality hit him.

Already homesick and afraid, he quelled the impulse to jump overboard and swim for shore.

"Was that your family?"

Gripping the handrail, Kyle watched the tiny figures as they headed back to the jetty where the speedboat was tied up. He was still wet from the spray getting here. They'd be soaked to the skin when they got home. A sob rose to his throat.

"If you're going to have an anxiety attack, come and sit down. Put your head between your knees."

"Wha— at?"

"I said, if you—"

"I heard you the first time," he snapped, turning on her.

"Keep your hair on, Red. I'm only trying to help." She looked back at him, a mild expression in her dark eyes. Her skin was the colour of milky coffee. She had silver piercings on both eyebrows and bottom lip. A turquoise gem winked from the side of her nose, and her hair was like tiny, coiled, black snakes. He had never seen anyone like her before in his life.

Uncertain how to respond, he shrugged and turned back to the sea.

"D'you want a coffee?" she asked as if he had a hearing problem. "I said—"

"I heard you. Okay, okay." Once she had gone, he found a quiet bench in the stern and settled his rucksack and holdall beside him. High above, the gulls screamed and dived in the ship's wake, reminding him of his final walk on Dave's beach with Aaron. He had blurted out his fears, embarrassed himself by breaking down, and Aaron had hugged him and told him he was brave and doing the right thing.

"Great seat, Red."

For a second, he wanted to strangle her.

"It's really crammed on the other side where the sun is." She held out a takeaway cup with a lid. "I brought sugar and milk."

He accepted it with an ungracious grunt.

"Wow, you've a lot of luggage. I've just got this." She swung a small, pink rucksack on to the floor at her side where it rustled against her long, gauzy, black skirt. "I'm hoping I can find someone in my size—"

"Look, what d'you want?" He snapped and was sorry when she looked like he'd slapped her. "I . . . I just need to be alone."

"So you can feel miserable in peace?"

"Something like that." He shrugged and turned back to watch the sky.

"I know where you're going," she sang.

He snorted in derision.

"Crannog."

He turned and, for the first time, noticed her beauty. All the makeup and metal couldn't hide her delicate features, her sparkling eyes. Her small-boned hands clutching the coffee cup were decorated with silver rings and rust-coloured tattoos. As he stared, her eyes seemed to narrow and take on a speculative glint. His stomach jerked. "Who are you? How d'you know about me?"

"Hey, cool it, Red. I'm Lola, and it's my second time. You've that scared rabbit look I've seen before with newbies."

"You've been before?"

She nodded, hair bouncing with the movement. "Didn't take the first time."

"What d'you mean?"

"You'll see." She dropped her empty cup, opened the drawstrings of her small velvet handbag and lifted out a battered tobacco tin. "Want one?" She asked, holding the open tin towards him.

Kyle shook his head. "What d'you mean, I'll see?" He watched her light a roll-up. The smell was unmistakeable. He quickly looked around, but there was no-one in sight. "What d'you think you're doing?"

"Having a relaxing smoke. Want a draw?"

"No way." He began to gather his stuff together.

"What're they gonna do, throw me off the ship? Radio ahead and have the police waiting? Cool it, Red." She smiled and patted his arm. "I'll put it out, ok?" She did what she said and put the remains back in the tin. "How old are you?" she smiled. "Fifteen, sixteen?"

"Eighteen," he snapped. "Not that it's any of your business."

"You look younger."

He shrugged; the bane of his life.

"And you're gay."

"No I'm not." Heat rose to his face, and he looked away from her knowing smile.

"Okay, whatever. I don't give a shit, but you need to be careful on the island."

He looked at her.

"Don't panic. I'll help you, but there's a guy called Alec. He's a bully."

Relief flooded through him. He had dealt with bullies before in school.

"He thinks he runs the place. He's homophobic, racist, sexist and every other kind of ist you can think of."

"Can't someone report him?"

She shrugged meaningfully. "People are scared, and he can get you things."

"Drugs you mean?"

"And booze and other things. He has contacts on the mainland." She tapped the side of her nose where the gem winked. "He'll notice you, Red, 'cause you're new and let's face it, you do look a bit gay."

"Sod off." He walked to the gunwale and threw his half full coffee towards the white froth below. "And stop calling me Red. My name's Kyle."

"Sorry." She came up to his side. "I'm not meaning to disrespect you, Kyle. But you are very good-looking. Haven't you had guys hitting on you in the past?"

Kyle mulled over what she said, trying to reconcile it with the reality. A vision of Nick with his scarred face and desperate apology filled his mind, and he shrugged. "A bit," he murmured.

"I'm going to the loo. Watch my bag." And she was gone in a flurry of skirts.

Kyle returned to the bench, wondering if he would let anybody down if he got the same ferry back home. Everyone had gone to so much trouble, protecting him, looking after him. He still couldn't get his head around why these people he'd only known a few months were more accepting, more affectionate towards him, than anyone he'd ever known. Well, maybe his mum, but he couldn't remember much about her, beyond a cloud of red hair and a scent. Was that what it was like? Having a family who looked out for you? He wanted to look out for them too, especially Aaron. He worried about him, back in Glasgow with Bill's people still on the loose.

A young couple wandered past, hand in hand, then returned to ask him to take their photograph against the blue sky. They handed him an iPad, very like the one Evie had given him, and showed him where to click the button.

As the ship began to turn, Lola came back and leaned over the rail. "Come and see." She pointed to the horizon on their right. "That's it, that's Craig Isle where Crannog House is."

As he reached the rail, the ship rocked with the change in angle, and the wind whistled though his hair.

"See these two pieces of land jutting out?" She pointed again. "There used to be huge metal rings dug into the ground on either side, with a chain attached. They'd drag it over to protect the harbour from pirates or invaders."

"Who did?"

"A princess, long ago."

He snorted. "That's just a fairy-tale."

"How you do know?"

The land grew closer, a lot of green fringed with gold. "How often does the ferry run?"

"Twice a week in summer, less in the winter, depending on the weather."

When they disembarked, Lola indicated the car parked on the quay. "That'll be for us."

Taken aback, Kyle looked at the shining vehicle. He was sure she'd made a mistake until a man in a chauffeur uniform got out and walked towards them. Despite himself, Kyle tensed. Chauffeurs in shiny, black cars had never preluded anything positive before. Lola was chattering on as she handed her rucksack to the chauffeur. She winked at him, called him "Andy", and they exchanged smiles.

"Welcome back, Miss Lola."

"This is Kyle, don't know his second name."

"Mr. MacLean," Andy said before Kyle could. "You're expected too, sir."

Kyle muttered a reply and watched as his luggage was whisked off to the car.

Lola flashed him a grin before climbing in.

Chapter Twenty-six

Kyle looked around in surprise. Although he'd had a tour of the main buildings during his assessment, it had consisted mainly of activity areas. The visitor's cabin he'd stayed in had been spotless and comfortable but nothing like the main building, which made him think of a fancy hotel he'd seen on TV. The reception was staffed by two beautiful young women in white coats with matching white smiles. In his jeans, grey hoodie and trainers, he felt inadequate and shy and the feeling persisted as he climbed the thickly carpeted staircase. His room was on the first floor, and if his room in Aaron's house had amazed him, this was an even greater shock.

It looked freshly decorated in muted shades of blue and green, white paintwork gleaming. The double bed, sofa and armchair facing a TV unit looked comfortable, while the wardrobe, chest of drawers and desk were pristine. His luggage lay beneath a window.

"Like it?" Bee asked. She was the Project Leader, Jake's wife and a therapist. He hoped she'd be his. She had a warm, engaging smile, and a mass of golden hair which refused to stay within its clips and bands.

"It . . . it's amazing. I never expected anything like this."

She smiled. "Through there is your en-suite bathroom and here," she said opening another door, "is your kitchen. You'll have your main meals in the refectory, but you can make snacks, drinks and so on in here."

He liked the red microwave, kettle and toaster and opened the tiny fridge to reveal milk, butter, fruit juice and bottled water. There were marked containers for bread, biscuits, coffee and sugar, and a cupboard above held dishes. He was amazed and felt quite humble. "Thank you so much."

"Each floor has two maids, so your kitchen will be restocked, and rooms will be cleaned regularly. The maids will change your bed, but you're expected to do your personal laundry. There's a timetable downstairs. And finally," she said, "no alcohol or illicit substances are allowed. Anyone found in possession will be asked to leave." She paused and he thought of Lola. Her brow wrinkled. "Do you drink?"

A memory surfaced. The sensation of glass hard against his teeth, raw whisky burning his mouth and throat. Laughter when he choked. He felt sick. "Hate the stuff," he muttered.

"I'm glad to hear it. People come here to heal, and it's hard enough without mood altering substances getting in the way."

His apprehension returned.

"Don't worry, Kyle." She patted his shoulder as she walked to the door. "Everyone's nervous at first. I'll leave you to unpack.

Supper's at six, and we'll sort out your programme in the morning."

As he found places for everything, Kyle thought of the programme he had discussed during his visit.

"You'll be kept busy," Jake, the project leader had said. He was a tall, bearded, athletic looking man with an air of authority which made Kyle nervous. "Physical activity is good for trauma recovery."

Jake had gone on to describe sessions ranging from gardening and taking part in walking groups to gym workouts and swimming. There was also art therapy, twice weekly individual counselling sessions, group work and massage, all of which Jake said, were 'mandatory'.

Kyle shuddered at the thought of someone's hands rubbing at his body and talking about his past in a group of people seemed equally impossible. He wasn't sure he could even do it with one person, unless it was Aaron. No matter what horrors he had stumbled and stammered into the light, Aaron had never flinched, had always insisted he was not to blame, no matter what they had made him do.

The knock on the door jerked him out of his reverie.

"Who is it?" he called.

"It's only me, Red," The door half opened and Lola's hair appeared. "Can I come in?"

"Okay."

She danced into the room and sat on the desk, legs swinging.

"Hey! You like science fiction," she exclaimed, flicking through his precious books. "I've got the Asimov robot books, if they haven't thrown them out. We could swop. Who's Aaron?" She pulled the little card from inside a book.

"My friend." Annoyed, Kyle took the card from her and slid it into a drawer. "Can you sit on the sofa please?"

"Sure." She laughed and complied.

He tidied his books back into a straight line again, spines outermost.

"Did he give you the books? Is he your boyfriend?"

"No. I told you, he's my friend."

"But you are gay, aren't you? You're too handsome to be straight. You remind me of a boy I saw once playing Romeo in a play."

"Why is it so important to you?" he snapped, annoyed at her persistence.

"No reason." Lola shrugged, smoothing her skirt. "We're all who we're meant to be." She glanced up at him. "I'm bi-sexual, thought I was lesbian, but I like guys too." She paused, and her mouth twisted. "Well, depending on the guys."

He didn't know how to respond.

"Personally," she continued, crossing her bare legs. "I prefer gay men to straight men any day."

He searched for something to say. He didn't have much experience with girls and she was like some sort of exotic species he had never encountered before. "I think that's a bit of a stereotype," he finally said, and when she looked at him enquiringly, he elaborated. "That all gay men are good looking. It's not true."

Lola's eyebrows rose, and she opened her mouth, then changed her mind and jumped to her feet. "Come on, Red. I'll give you the tour."

<>

Outside in the quadrangle, where people were reading and chatting on benches, Lola pointed out the gym and swimming pool, which seemed busy. "And over there." She indicated a smaller building with firmly closed double doors. "Is where you get your massages and things. Thai, Swedish, Aromatherapy. They're supposed to relax you. Had the opposite effect on me."

"How long were you here?" he asked when he could.

"A while, and over there's the kitchen and refectory. Everyone eats together, and the grubs's good."

"Yes, I remember."

She rounded on him, eyes narrowed. "I thought you were new?"

She was so aggressive, he stepped back. "I am, but I came for a week's assessment." She remained staring, so he moved away and sat on a bench beside a white urn overflowing with small multi-coloured flowers.

A shadow blocked the sun. Tall and dark, the man's long Persian eyes were magnetising.

Kyle grinned. "How're you doing, Navin?"

"I've been looking for you all day," Navin's smile was gentle. His gaze was frankly admiring, but with none of the aggressive hunger Nick had displayed. "The Sunday ferries don't always run to time."

Kyle smiled back and turned to Lola. "Nav was my buddy during my assessment. He took care of me."

"I'm sure he did," she chuckled, in a sudden mood change. "Well, I'll leave you boys to get reacquainted. See you at supper, maybe."

Chapter Twenty-seven

Meals were noisy, colourful affairs where everyone ate together at tables laid with shining cutlery, glasses and cloth napkins. The food was self-service from hot and cold tables, displaying plentiful dishes of every description. Although his time with Aaron had introduced him to a wider palate than he'd been used to, Kyle felt lost by the choices at supper and had simply copied Navin. This led to his first experience of a real curry; not the takeaways he'd shared with the boys in the flat. Navin had been so overjoyed at his responses to various flavours bursting on his tongue, you'd have thought he'd cooked it himself.

Breakfast choices were easier, although Kyle couldn't understand why anyone would want to eat fish in the morning. With a loaded tray, he followed Navin to the same table they had used at supper and was relieved to find the same occupants, apart from Lola who didn't seem to be eating breakfast. He noticed that Andrew, a tall, lanky ginger, who talked a lot, seemed to be friends with Craig, a smaller, intense guy with a stutter, although they never stop arguing. The other two occupants were girls. Ayeesha, quiet and very feminine, with shining dark hair and skin, and Sal, a chunky looking girl with short blonde hair and a chin and mouth which Kyle thought shouted determination and stubbornness. He liked her on sight.

"We don't know if that's the reason he left," Andrew argued as they sat down.

"Well it s–s–seems likely," Craig replied.

Kyle half listened as he dug in to his fried breakfast, accepting Navin's offerings of salt and pepper; a roll and butter, then milk and sugar when coffee was served by a stern-looking waitress. All Navin seemed to need was a smile of thanks for his dark cheeks to take on a rosy glow. Kyle checked out the room as he ate. For his own survival, he had become well-practiced at reading people and noted, among the hubbub, the quiet people who sat with heads down and the ones who seemed to be in charge.

A couple of tables away, a man caught his attention. He seemed to be holding court with a small audience apparently drinking in his words. As if aware of Kyle's gaze, the man looked around at him. His eyes narrowed as he focused and even at this distance, Kyle could sense an air of menace. Something about his thin face and crew cut hair reminded Kyle of the school bullies who made the smaller boys lives a misery. Determined not to be intimidated, Kyle grit his teeth, and held his gaze, until the man looked away.

"Are you okay?" Eyes troubled, Navin brought him back.

"I'm fine, just day-dreaming." He put the remainder of his bacon on a roll and began to munch it. The waitress returned with more coffee.

"Thanks, Tricia," Andrew said to her before turning back to Craig. "What other reason would they make you leave? It must be about his fees."

Cup halfway to his mouth, Kyle froze. "What fees?" The whole table stared at him.

"The fees for staying here?" Andrew frowned.

"I . . . I didn't know there were fees."

Craig snorted. "Eight th-thousand a m-month minimum!"

Afraid his breakfast would come back up, Kyle swallowed hard and took some deep breaths. "No-one mentioned money." He looked from Andrew's confusion to the incredulity reflected in Craig's eyes. The chauffeur-driven car; the huge, main building in its own grounds, with its turrets and Scottish flag, the state-of-the-art gym and swimming pool, the accommodation – of course it all had to be paid for. How the hell did he imagine it was free? *What an idiot I am,* he thought. *I need to tell them.* He pushed back his chair.

Navin stopped him with a hand on his arm. "Be calm," he said.

"They've made a mistake. I need to tell them."

Navin smiled. "Don't worry, Kyle. It will be alright."

"But you don't understand. I don't have any money," Kyle confessed. He rose and walked blindly past tables full of people with more money than he could ever dream of. When he reached Bee's office, it was empty, so he stood outside and waited.

After a few minutes she arrived with Jake, both talking animatedly. "What's happened, Kyle?" she asked in concern. "You look like you've seen a ghost."

"I . . . I can't stay," Kyle blurted. "I'm here under false pretences."

They both gazed in concern and, as people began to walk along the corridor, Jake put an arm around his shoulder and guided him into his wife's room. He sat him in a comfortable chair while Bee poured him some water.

"Now," Jake said, sitting beside him, "tell me what's troubling you."

Kyle told him the whole story; from his first visit with Owen, through his assessment, to what he had heard at the breakfast table, realising as he did so how much he wanted to stay. "And I don't have any money to pay you," he finished in a small voice. He didn't know quite what to expect, but it wasn't Jake's amusement.

The man's face creased into a grin, eyes dancing with amusement, then his gaze softened. "Is that all?" he asked. "We do have a couple of free places, but . . . ?" He looked at his wife, now seated at her computer.

"Paid six months in advance," Bee declared, "by Aaron Douglas."

Kyle stared at her in shock. "Aaron doesn't have that kind of money. There must be a mistake."

"See for yourself." She turned the computer screen towards him.

"Why would he do that? I'll have to phone him."

"One explanation," said Jake, "is that he cares for you a great deal and wants you to get better."

Kyle blinked against the threatening tears.

"And as for phoning him." Bee raised an eyebrow and handed him his timetable. "Do that later, huh? According to this, you're supposed to be in the gym."

<>

It was in the evening before he got a chance to phone Aaron. He'd had a busy, active day, hadn't felt like supper, and had retired to his room for some quiet time.

"I didn't tell you, because I didn't want you to feel indebted to me," Aaron explained.

"But, how, how can you afford it?" He heard Aaron's familiar chuckle.

"I didn't take out a loan, if that's what you're worried about."

There was silence for a few minutes. All that Kyle could hear across the miles was the creaking of the old desk chair, which Aaron had told him had belonged to his dad, a poet who had died too young. "I think I mentioned my parents split up when my sister and I were ten," Aaron said. "Our mother went home to France. We visited during school holidays, but she was killed in a skiing accident when we were fifteen. Her family is well off, and she left us a fair bit of money."

"That much?"

"And a great deal more," Aaron said. "This isn't for you to worry about. You're there to recover, so you can move on with your life."

"Jake said," Kyle ventured. "You probably did it because you care about me a lot and want me to get better." He listened in the silence to Aaron's breathing.

"Well, then, he must be right," Aaron said in his ear. "He's a famous doctor with lots of letters after his name. So how was your first day?"

"It was good. Listen Aaron, thanks so much. I'll never forget this," Kyle said in a rush. "I'll . . . I'll pay you back one day."

"Okay, that's a deal. Remember to e-mail Evie. She'll be desperate to know how you got on today."

After he'd sent Aaron's sister a message, showered and prepared for an early night, Kyle answered a tentative knock on his door.

Navin stood there with a tray. "Brought you some supper. Can I come in?"

"I'll put the kettle on." Kyle smiled, stepping back.

Although he hadn't thought he was hungry, he demolished the food in a remarkably short time and sat back with a coffee.

"They were talking about the guy who's left again at supper," Navin said from the chair where he sat with his own drink. "He was apparently smoking dope. Andy the chauffeur caught him hanging about the barn."

Kyle heard the news with surprise and slight relief. "Nothing to do with his fees, then?"

Navin shook his head. "Did you get through to Aaron?"

"Yes, it's right enough. He has money his mum left him. I told him I'd pay him back one day and I will."

"He's a good friend."

"Awesome." Kyle finished his coffee and stretched out with a sigh.

Navin leaned across and placed his own empty mug on the coffee table. "You should never worry about money, Kyle. I have plenty."

Surprised, Kyle stared at him. "What do you mean?"

Navin shrugged, his cheeks glowing. "I have lots of money. Far too much just for me." He smiled in the shy way he had. "I . . . I told you why I'm here?"

"Yes, your family died in an accident." Kyle nodded sadly, unable to comprehend the horror of it.

"It was two years ago. We were on holiday and the caravan blew up when I was out walking the dog. My parents and both my little brothers died." Navin's voice trembled. "I still feel guilty. It's called survivor guilt."

He sighed, and Kyle sat up and stretched a hand towards him. Navin grabbed it and squeezed. "I'm okay, really, I'm working through it bit by bit."

His shoulders lifted in a half shrug. "There was a fault with the bottled gas in the caravan and I received a lot of compensation. It just made the guilt feelings worse, so I made the decision that I'd do some good with it and help people." He smiled. "I made sure my grandparents were okay—they're dead now and left it all back to me. So, I invested some, gave some to charity and all that, but there's lots left, so anything you need, anything at all."

Overcome, Kyle let his strong, warm hand go and sat back. "What can I say, Nav? First Aaron, now, you . . . why is all this happening to me?" He tried to pull himself together. "You're very kind, but why would you? I . . . I mean, you don't really know me very well."

Navin smiled and looked down at the table. "I know you well enough and . . . and I like you."

Uncertain what to say or do, Kyle settled for piling dishes and mugs on to the tray. "I'd better wash these up."

Navin stopped him with a hand on his forearm. "Don't be scared, I'll never, ever hurt you." Sincerity radiated from his warm gaze and Kyle gulped against the annoying tears again.

"What is it about this place?" He tried to laugh. "I can't stop crying."

Navin gave his arm a squeeze. "Healing tears," he said, as he lifted the tray and headed for the kitchen.

Chapter Twenty-eight

Bill's face dominated the room.

The light was off and the huge, wall-mounted TV flickered with the movements on screen. Transfixed, Kyle clung to the door-jamb. He had simply glanced through the open door as he passed, on his way to bed, when the awful sight caught his eye.

Bill was standing in front of Glasgow High Court while reporters reached towards him with their microphones. Behind him clustered a group of men in suits, one of whom was reading from a clipboard. On the edge, as if cast adrift, was a small, very pretty woman who clutched a bright red handbag to her chest like a shield. From photographs on Bill's desk, Kyle recognised her as his very young wife.

Kyle forced himself into the TV lounge. Only one person was there; a woman from his therapy group curled in an armchair. She looked up when he moved into the room.

"Hi, Kyle."

"Hi, Manda. D'you mind if I turn this up for a few minutes?"

"Help yourself. I'm just waiting for my programme to start after the news." She smiled as she handed him the remote control.

He pressed the control too hard and the voice of his nightmares boomed through the room. "Sorry, Manda." He lowered the sound.

"Of course I'm shocked." Bill said in that pseudo-sincere voice Kyle remembered with a shudder. "Shocked and saddened that someone would tell those lies about me." His voice rose, and the man with the clipboard raised a hand as if to silence him. "I spend my life trying to help people, but even I have enemies."

"Who do you think your enemies are, Bill?" asked a female reporter, thrusting her microphone forward."

Bill looked at her with a serious expression and slowly shook his head. "Who knows, my dear, but I'll find out."

"Are you going to withdraw your candidacy for election, Bill?" A voice asked from the jostling crowd.

"Never!" Bill seemed to glare straight at Kyle, chin raised in defiance. "Never! People know me. My constituents know me. Our wonderful police force will get to the bottom of these terrible accusations and they'll be dealt with."

Manda laughed. "Sounds like Winston Churchill. Never in the field of . . . " She looked up at Kyle, clutching the back of a sofa for support. "Are you alright?"

Kyle realised he was shaking from head to foot. He was scared to let go, in case he collapsed. "N—not so good."

She jumped up immediately and flung an arm around his shoulders. "Come and sit down."

He couldn't take his eyes off the screen as Bill continued to rant. He was aware of Manda taking the remote control and turning down the sound.

"Come over, sit on the couch. Should I get Bee, or Nav or somebody?"

Kyle shook his head as she gently towed him across and sat him down. He was sweating, struggling to breathe. He knew what was happening, but couldn't do a damn thing to stop it.

"Wait there." He heard her say as he began to fade.

Sometime later, he became aware of a warm hand on his frozen chest, another supporting the small of his back and Jake's calm voice in his ear. "Well done, Kyle. You're doing fine. Just breathe."

On his knees before him, holding his hands, sat Nav, eyes filled with tears.

"Good boy." Jake's quiet voice steadied him. "Big, deep breaths."

Kyle moved his fingers in Navin's warm grasp.

"Are you okay?" Tears ran down Navin's flushed cheeks.

Kyle nodded and breathed.

"There you go now." Jake patted his shoulder as he let him go. "Well done, how do you feel?"

"Fine, thank you."

Jake huffed a quiet laugh. "What a polite young man. Do you want a drink?" He pointed Navin to the glass of water on a nearby table.

Kyle took a sip, felt a raging thirst, swallowed the lot and felt a sudden need to sleep.

"Bed, I think," Jake pronounced. "Can you stay with him, Navin?"

"Of course."

"Don't hesitate to phone if you're worried."

With a start of fright, Kyle woke. For a few moments he lay disorientated. He was in bed, the room dimly lit, but he wasn't alone. He jerked upright. Nav sprawled on the couch, head back, mouth wide, snoring fit to lift the roof. The sight made Kyle feel safe. He lay back with a sigh and drifted off again.

Chapter Twenty-nine

Kyle halted in his usual spot at the cliff edge and retrieved the water bottle from his backpack. Breathless from climbing up from the beach, he gulped too fast and broke into a fit of coughing. So out of condition, he thought, but it was good to be running again, feeling his weakened muscles stretch and toughen.

It had been raining earlier, and the grass was damp, but he was already wet with sweat, so he sat on it anyway and dangled his legs over the edge. He munched an apple and gazed out to sea. On the grey horizon was a ship he thought would be making for its mainland port. Tiny dots swooped and dived in its wake, reminding him of being in Port Peter with Dave, watching the fishing boats coming into the sheltered harbour. Sometimes, he missed staying at Dave's, cosy and safe in the big old-fashioned bedroom with the hypnotic flash of the nearby lighthouse beacon sending him to sleep. Then, he remembered the nightmares which never seemed to stop no matter where he was living.

His thoughts drifted to the earlier therapy session. The first few had been easy. Bee had focussed on helping him manage his anxiety by teaching him breathing techniques and relaxation exercises. This morning, everything had changed.

"When something bad happens to you," she said, "you have three choices. You can let it define you, let it destroy you, or let it strengthen you." She'd paused and smiled, blue eyes twinkling. "You're already strong and resilient, or you wouldn't be here." Her brows furrowed as she became serious. "But you have a lifetime of pain bottled up inside you, Kyle. It leaks through your nightmares and causes panic attacks, like when you saw that man on television the other week." She paused again as he took that in. "Do you understand what I'm saying?"

It didn't require much thought. He nodded.

"You've told me how you've self-harmed in the past and that's nothing to be ashamed of."

Kyle frowned and looked down at the floor.

"It's a way of managing the internal pain, of coping, but you've moved from cutting your arms and thighs to your stomach, and that's more serious." She stopped again and leaned forward in her chair. "If you're ready, we're going to shake that bottle. It won't be easy and there will be times when you'll want to pack it all in and go home, but if you work hard and use all the supports available, you *will* recover. I guarantee it."

She waited as he traced the pattern on the rug between them with his foot. *I'm here to get better*, he thought. *I can't go on the way things are. One day I might just do it.* Someone had shown him once where to cut the big vein in his neck. It was easy. He looked up to compassionate eyes and nodded.

A few words, a bit of guided thinking and his brain exploded in a kaleidoscope of pictures. He was back there. Held down over a desk as Bill 'broke in' his ten-year-old body. He'd howled again and again, and was violently sick into Bee's waiting basin.

She had nurtured and supported him back to reality, but as he left, she had warned him to take things easy and stay around other people as he might experience another flashback later in the day. The ghost of the memory made him shift uncomfortably on the grass.

"Hi there," said a voice. "Don't you fall now, will you?"

His stomach lurched as a hand grabbed his shoulder and did a push/pull movement. "Gerr-off," he yelled, trying to scrabble backwards. He was shoved forward again, wet grass sliding beneath him. A yelp escaped him, and he heard a mocking laugh.

"Cool it, pretty boy. I thought you liked a strong hand."

Released, Kyle struggled to his feet and squared up to the bully, fists clenched. "What the fuck, you stupid bastard!"

"Now, now." The man parodied jumping back, hands raised as if defending himself. "There's no need for that language. It was just a game."

"I don't think he likes your games, Alec," said another voice as he was shoved forward.

Off balance, he staggered almost into Alec's arms, so close he could smell the man's rancid breath. He was pushed back again and so it went on, both men roaring with laughter as he skittled back and forth between them.

He fought, but it was happening too fast, and his trainers wouldn't grip. Panic rose, his chest strained to reach a breath. Memories crowded in and he was back there again with terrible clarity.

They had stripped him, hard, rough hands tugging at his clothes. He was naked and crying when they ridiculed his child's body and called him 'Tiny Tim'. "On your knees, boy," a voice instructed. "You've work to do."

Chapter Thirty

Lola saw them from the top of the rise, dancing around something on the ground. As she got closer she recognised them—Alec and his nutter—pal, Stan 'the man', who was usually high on something. Not wanting to get involved, she hesitated and made to turn back.

"Hey, Lola baby," a voice shouted.

"Fuck." She made a half-hearted wave and started down the hill towards them.

"What's happening, baby-doll?" Stan leered as she grew closer. As usual his long hair looked greasy, and he needed a shave.

"Piss off," she spat.

They were standing over what appeared to be a pile of clothes. "What's this, Alec? A rain dance?" She asked.

He grinned in response, reached over to stroke her cheek and laughed when she flinched. "Cool it, baby. You aren't so smart when you need what I got."

Before she could reply, the pile of clothes moved and groaned. Puzzled, she bent closer. The curled body shuddered, and she glimpsed a flash of copper hair. "Kyle?" She dropped to her knees beside him. "Are you alright? What've you done to him, Alec?"

"Haven't done a thing. We were just talking and the wee cunt fell flat on his face."

With a disbelieving look, Lola bent over Kyle and touched his head. His body curled into a tighter ball. She rounded on Alec again. "What did you do?"

"We didn't do nothing," Stan denied. "Maybe he wanted us to—do something," he said with an exaggerated wink. "So he's gone in a wee queerie huff."

"Don't be stupid," she began, but he was hurrying in Alec's wake, off down the path towards the Centre.

After a moment, Kyle groaned and blinked as if he was waking up.

"Hey, sweetheart," she whispered, supporting him to sit. "Are you alright?"

He scrubbed his face with his hands and muttered something.

"Did they hurt you?"

"Who?"

"Alec and Stan. They were here a minute ago."

Kyle squeezed his eyes shut and shook his head.

"Don't you remember?" Lola watched him in concern. "They were both here."

"I know, I remember. They didn't do anything, well, just pushed me around a bit."

She grabbed him as he staggered to his feet.

"I'm okay. Thanks, I'm okay." Freckles stood out like bright stars on the pale skin of his face. He was shaking, and his tracksuit was soaked and covered in muddy grass-stains.

"You don't look it." She reached for her phone. "I'll text Nav to come meet us."

"No, for God's sake. Nav'll come in an ambulance, or something. I'm okay, really. I just flipped. Bee warned me it might happen." He grabbed a half-full water bottle from the ground and took a drink.

Casting around, Lola retrieved his backpack from the cliff edge. "Is that the first time they've harassed you?"

"Don't worry about it." He accepted his bag with a nod of thanks. "I've coped with a lot worse than them. Keep this to yourself. I don't want everybody to know."

She hesitated. "You promise to tell Bee?"

He nodded in a resigned way.

Chapter Thirty-one

Head down as he chuckled over a text Stuart had sent, Kyle almost walked into someone.

"Watch it, queer."

He jerked up his head and stared into Stan's sneering face. Before he could respond, Lola appeared from nowhere.

"I know you won't do much reading, Stan," she said, "but the LGBTQ community have now adopted the word queer as their own." She smiled sweetly. "So, it's no longer an insult to call someone queer."

"Fuck off, bitch."

"That's another one," she called at his retreating back. "Going to supper, Kyle?"

They looked around the busy refectory for a seat. Kyle noticed Nav waving from a table in the centre of the busy room and headed towards him.

"How did your session go this morning?" Nav asked, when Kyle sat beside him.

Kyle made a face. "Cried like a baby."

"Good session, then," Lola commented, rolling her eyes. "That's how they judge it, anyway." She sniffed. "Never made me cry."

With a shake of his head, Kyle let it go and tucked into his meal. In the therapy group they shared, Lola had divulged some of her abusive background, and he understood her need to appear tough and in control. His earlier fears about not being able to share in a group had dissipated, with his only problem now being that Stan was also a member.

Ayeesha and Sal joined them and Kyle smiled in greeting, but neither responded. He exchanged a puzzled glance with Navin.

"Hey, guys," Lola said, "how're you both doing? Haven't seen you in a couple of days."

Long, dark eyelashes fluttered as Ayeesha looked down at the table, but Sal raised her head with a determined gaze. "Alec tried it on with her."

Kyle was immediately concerned. He knew the Asian girl had escaped a forced marriage and had been discovered sleeping rough and starving by the Glasgow police. Her story, when she'd stammered it out in the group, had left some members in tears. Before he could speak, Lola was in there.

"That bastard needs it cut off with rusty shears."

"Who's that, then?" Andrew asked cheerfully, lowering his loaded tray with a bang. "Hi, everybody, sorry I'm late. Alan in the gym was showing me and Craig a few self-defence moves." He stopped and looked around. "What's going on?"

Craig joined them, equally noisy with his tray until Andrew hushed him.

"Sal's just said that swine Alec tried it on with Ayeesha," Lola informed them, her face twisted with disgust.

"Wh-what d-did he do?" Craig asked, innocent gaze magnified by his owlish glasses.

Sal glared, and Ayeesha hid behind her curtain of shining hair.

"S-s-sorry."

"Shut it, Craig," Andrew murmured and raised his voice. "He punched me in the stomach once when I wouldn't give him protection money, and Tommy in the room next to me said that creep Stan nearly broke his thumb."

Kyle was aghast. "Protection money?" Navin's glance told a story. "You too?"

Navin grimaced

"You can't fight back," Andrew said.

Still watching Navin, Kyle was indignant. "Why not? He's not that big."

"Two against one," Lola said with a knowing look.

Aware of Navin's questioning gaze, Kyle squirmed with embarrassment. "They caught me this afternoon, and I, well I sort of flipped," he said, waiting for the inevitable response.

"What do you mean? What did they do to you?" Navin's voice was uncharacteristically loud and his eyes had darkened.

Taken aback by his vehemence, Kyle patted his arm. "I'm okay. It was nothing. They just pushed me about a bit, and I had a stupid flashback. Bee warned me it might happen."

Navin's eyes widened, but before he could respond, Lola butted in with an apologetic glance at Kyle. "I found him curled in a ball on the ground."

"What the fuck, Kyle?"

It was the first time Kyle had heard Nav swear, and the shock made him hesitate too long.

"That's it. You aren't going running on your own again." Navin said flatly. "We'll get our timetables changed and I'll come with you."

"You couldn't keep up."

"I can get fitter."

"Will you guys stop arguing?" Sal interrupted. "We have to do something about this."

"Like what?" Navin asked, his colour still high.

"Kick him in the nuts," Lola hissed.

"T-tell J-Jake."

"No," Ayeesha begged. "Please, no. He will throw me out."

Sal silenced the denials. "She thinks Jake won't believe her over Alec."

"He . . . he said I'm just a freebie," Ayeesha said as if confessing a sin.

"So's he." Andrew's tone was indignant. "Came out in the group. He's a fuckin' charity case." He winced. "Sorry, Ayeesha, I didn't mean—"

"It is alright, Andrew." Her smile was gentle. "I, too, am a charity case."

"So am I," Kyle challenged. "Do you have a problem with that?"

"No, sorry mate." Andrew blushed and gestured as if to calm things down. "I didn't mean it the way it sounded."

"For God's sake," Sal said, exasperated. "Who cares? What're we going to do?"

Various voices joined in, until the table hushed like a tree full of birds when a predator was close. Kyle looked up. Tray in hand, Alec had paused at their table. A sneer twisted his mouth as he stared at them one by one. When he reached Ayeesha's cowering form, he slowly smiled and winked. Sal reared up until Andrew dragged her back down. "Enjoy your supper," Alec said as he left, closely followed by a sniggering Stan.

There was a collective release of breath.

"I thought he was going to rape me," Ayeesha whispered in the silence.

Kyle took it like a punch to his throat. He watched the girl squeeze her eyes closed and pull her hair over her face and he thought of other humiliated young faces he'd seen over the years. He glared across the room at Alec where he now sat wolfing his meal; the same monster, a different face. His body began to shake as rage boiled up, and he was half out of his chair before Nav grabbed his arm.

"What're you doing, Ky?"

The rage slid back to a simmer, and he resumed his seat. He swallowed hard, jaw aching from clenching his teeth. "Let's sort this bastard. Who's with me?"

Chapter Thirty-two

He was drying himself after a shower when he heard his main door opening and Nav's voice.

"I'm in here, won't be a minute," He called back.

"You'll never believe what's happened." Nav appeared in the open bathroom doorway. He stopped and stared at Kyle's nakedness as if transfixed, his mouth half open.

Embarrassed, Kyle yanked a towel around his waist. He had suspected that Nav wanted him and, sometimes, he thought he wanted Nav too, but each time he thought about it, other faces loomed, teeth bared, laughing as they raped him.

"Excuse me." Nav blushed as he backed out.

"Give me a minute. Put the kettle on."

When he went through to the living room in pyjamas, Nav had made coffee and switched the TV on. He threw Kyle a sheepish glance before fiddling with the remote control. "What's wrong with this thing? I can't get the channel."

"Told you before, it takes turns. What is it you want to see?"

"The news. There's a bit about the Centre coming up. Hope we haven't missed it."

Kyle stopped hearing him as he gazed at the screen. He recognised the picture; knew when it had been taken, where he'd been standing making silly faces in an effort to make Nathan laugh. Then it had been his own turn to have a formal photograph taken for the school year-book and Nathan had returned the favour. From afar he heard the newsreader's words: "... *the headless body of the young man washed up on Irvine beach a week ago, has been identified as seventeen-year-old Nathan Briggs...*" before he passed out.

<>

When he came to, flat on his back, his vision was filled with Nav's handsome face, dark eyes clouded with concern. "What is it?" Nav whispered. "What can I do?"

Without conscious volition Kyle reached for him and buried his face against his chest. With an inarticulate murmur, Nav gathered him close. They stayed like that for some time as Kyle struggled to expunge the horror from his mind. He was conscious of the reassuring solidity and warmth of Nav's body and the steady heartbeat in his ear.

"Are you alright?"

Kyle had to work saliva into his mouth before he could speak. "Headless . . . " he croaked. "They chopped his head off." He shut his eyes and hung on to Nav, but the picture in his brain was still vivid. The strong arms pulled him closer, and he could feel Nav's mouth against his forehead.

After a bit, Nav moved. "Did you know him?"

Kyle he raised his head and sat back on his heels. He felt sick. "Nathan was my friend. We shared a room for two years in the school." The tears came again and he closed his eyes. "Last I heard, he was working in one of Bill's brothels." Memories roared through his brain: Nathan's laughter; his ability to cheer him up with a corny joke, hanging out the window with him sharing a smoke and a stolen can of beer, or crouched in fear between their beds as doors slammed and names were called, praying they wouldn't be chosen. Once, Nathan had been so afraid he'd wet himself. A picture slithered through his brain: Nathan on his knees, head bowed while looming above, Bill with maniacal grin, raising a machete. "No, God, no." In an effort to erase it, Kyle scrubbed his hands over his face.

"Ky, I know this is horrible, but you need to tell someone."

"Tell who?"

Nav sighed. "Jake, or Aaron or even the police."

Kyle started to argue, then realising the sense in his words, stopped and bit his lip. "Okay, I'll phone Aaron," but when he tried the phone went to voicemail. "He's probably working. I'll try Dave."

Dave listened without interruption. "Hell, son," he responded. "I'm so damn sorry. I actually saw that news report. Are you okay?"

"Not really."

"Do you want to speak to Aaron?"

Kyle's heart leapt. "He's there? Aaron's there?"

"Yes, Aaron and Sandi are staying for a few days."

"Oh, it's okay. You just tell him," Kyle stammered, mood plummeting.

"Sandi's in bed. I'll get Aaron. Hang on."

Kyle heard footsteps, the inevitable squeak as the living room door opened and Dave called Aaron's name. After a moment, he could hear them conversing and the phone was exchanged.

"Kyle, are you okay?"

At the sound of the familiar voice, he wanted to cry again.

"Sure, I'm alright. It was the shock of seeing his picture on telly like that and hearing what . . . what they did to him."

"I can only imagine, horrific for you."

"I . . . just wanted to talk to you, let you know. I'm not sure what to do."

"Do you want me to come over? I could be there tomorrow."

Despite the sudden rush of emotion, Kyle hesitated. Although desperate to see Aaron's familiar face, his therapy was steadily changing the way he made decisions. "Thanks, but there's no need. I just wondered what you thought. If I should talk to the police?"

Aaron was silent, then Kyle heard him speaking to someone. Dave came back on.

"Yes, I think you should, Kyle. They obviously know who Nathan was, but your personal knowledge will help." Dave paused. "Do you want me to have a word with them?"

"Yes, thanks."

"Okay, I'll let you know what they say. I'll put Aaron back on."

"Good decision," Aaron said, when the phone was exchanged. "Do you have anyone you can trust to talk to about this?"

"Yes, Nav's here."

"Good, I'd like to meet him sometime."

"He'd like to meet you too." Kyle smiled as Nav came through from the kitchen with two mugs of hot chocolate. "He's a good friend." When he finished the phone call and half the chocolate, his mood dropped again.

"Would you like me to stay?" Nav asked. "The couch is very comfy."

Kyle looked into his kind eyes and nodded.

<>

The nightmare was horrendous; screams and laughter, Sean sobbing and Nathan's severed head begging him for help. As he surfaced, with raw throat and bitten tongue, he became aware of someone murmuring softly into his ear. Strong arms surrounded him.

"It's only me," Nav whispered, "You're safe, I've got you."

Chapter Thirty-three

Opening his eyes, Kyle stared into other eyes, so dark they were almost black. In the same moment he became aware of two undeniable facts; the insistent hardness against his thigh and the electric shock of his own arousal. An instant of blinding terror and he yanked himself back, almost falling out of bed.

"I'm sorry," Nav whispered, sliding away and clambering fully dressed to his feet.

Consumed by a fierce need for he knew not what, Kyle made a grab for his T-shirt and missed.

"Going for a pee," Nav said. "I'll put the kettle on."

Kyle lay there in a lather of confusion and shame. What if his body couldn't tell the difference between willing and unwilling sex? What if he had a flashback in the middle of it?

<>

"Well done, Andrew," Alan the gym coach said, "and you too, Sal." He paused at the end of the line, where Ayeesha stood. "No, lass, you have to keep your fingers straight when you stab into the throat. It isn't a tickle. Remember the idea is to disable him before you kick him in the nuts."

Ayeesha made a sound between a giggle and a squeak.

Kyle stepped forward from where he stood next to Nav and peered along at her. Despite sounding enthusiastic when self-defence was agreed to at their table, Ayeesha's entire body language screamed her unwillingness to participate. She looked so fragile next to Alan, who was unsuccessfully trying to shape delicate fingers into weapons.

"Maybe not the best exercise for her," Sal piped up, ever protective.

Alan looked ready to argue, then shrugged his wide shoulders and released Ayeesha. "Don't worry, lass. It's not for everyone." He looked at the others. "We'll need to leave it at that today, folks. See you next week. Tell Lola she was missed again and . . . "

"Don't stop practicing," they said in unison.

On the way to the changing area, they discussed Lola's absence.

"It's my study time, I'll visit her." Kyle volunteered.

"I'm due in therapy," Nav said before he left. "Promise me you won't go running."

Kyle looked into his earnest eyes and remembered the earlier heat between them. Something must have shown in his expression as Nav blushed and turned away.

"I won't, I promise," he said to Nav's retreating back. "See you later."

<>

Lola came to the door wrapped in a blanket, looking small and miserable.

"Can I come in?" Kyle asked, shocked at the sight of her.

She nodded, stepped back and returned to curl into the corner of the couch, which by the heaped cushions, blankets and used paper tissues, was her comfort zone. "Help yourself to coffee."

"Do you want one?"

She shook her head and burrowed beneath the blankets.

"What's up, Lola? Are you ill? Is it the flu?"

Without warning, she was sobbing, hiccupping and hiding beneath the blanket. Kyle rushed across and sat beside her, holding her until she began to calm, her cries becoming less desperate.

"What's wrong? What's happened?"

"Can't you tell?" She pushed away from him, grabbed a tissue and blew her nose hard. "Look at me."

Kyle scrutinised her messy hair and pale face with mascara streaks. "What am I supposed to look at?"

She jerked away. "For God's sake. You may be gay, but you're such a fucking bloke."

Confused, he watched her scrabble in a small velvet bag which lay beside her. Her normally perfect nail-varnish was chipped as she produced a mirror, grabbed a wad of tissues and scrubbed at the mascara smears with frantic movements. A sudden shaft of sunshine illuminated her sad face, pale and wan without lipstick. She shivered, and he pulled the blanket around her shoulders and in doing so, noticed her eyes. Her pupils were pinpoints.

"What have you taken?"

She shrugged, head lowered. "Nothing bad."

"What's that supposed to mean?"

Her head shot up in challenge. "What I said. I know what I'm doing."

"Do you?" Kyle held her gaze and felt lost when she began crying again. He had a vivid memory of being hugged so tightly as a child, he could scarcely breathe; the all-consuming helplessness of hearing a woman sobbing. Unable to handle the situation, he got up and switched on the kettle. As he loaded the mug with coffee and sugar, he tried to remember if this was the right thing to do. In school, people just came down again and felt low for days, or used weed to numb the effects.

She was snuffling into a tissue and delicately running a finger beneath her eyes.

He placed the mug on the coffee table and sat on the couch so he was facing her. "Where did you get it, Lola?"

She flicked him a look, her eyelashes stuck together in clumps.

"Just a guy."

"Which guy?"

She grabbed the coffee mug and gulped. "Gaads, how much sugar did you put in this?" but she drank it anyway.

He waited until she had put down the empty mug and burrowed back beneath the blankets, before asking the obvious question. "Is Alec your supplier?"

For a moment, she looked like she was about to argue, then her eyes closed, tears leaking down her cheeks. "I was doing ok," she whispered, "Then, one day he offered me a taste. That's all it takes for someone like me."

"Bastard," Kyle hissed.

She raised her head, gaze haunted. "I pay him in kind."

Kyle accepted the statement without demur. He had done things himself to stop worse things happening to him. "Does he hurt you?"

Her lips twisted in disgust. "He likes it rough. I'm just a whore."

"No, you aren't," Kyle said with vehemence. "You're an addict being exploited by a twisted bastard who preys on other people."

Lola stared at him. "I knew you were special the first moment I met you."

Embarrassed, he looked away. "Don't be daft."

"You are. People listen to you."

He dismissed her words with a shake of his head. "You can't go on like this. You have to stop."

Tears spilled through her poor, ruined eyelashes. "I . . . I need it."

"You can beat it."

"You don't understand."

In trying to find the right thing to say, Kyle remembered how Aaron had responded to his despair in the bad times. "You're a strong person, Lola – a fighter. You've survived so much in your life. Don't let this bastard beat you."

"I'm not strong."

"You're always fighting! You fight everybody and everything."

Her mouth twitched into a sad smile. "My therapist would say that's defensive behaviour."

"So what? It takes strength and courage to fight!"

She pulled the blanket cocoon closer. "I'm not what you think. It's all an act." Before he could respond she closed her eyes. "Let me sleep, Red, please, I'm knackered."

Chapter Thirty-four

Nothing might have happened if he hadn't walked across the quadrangle and seen Alec leaving the gym laughing as a young, black woman struggled in his embrace.

Kyle found himself running straight for him, yelling something at the top of his voice. Everything seemed to slow: the girl fleeing back towards the gym, Alec's wide-eyed shock, his mouth twisting with contempt when he recognised his assailant, then blossoming red when his head juddered under the impact of Kyle's punch.

Time sped up. Stan appeared, lashing out with both fists. Kyle felt a blow to his nose, heard a noise in his head like bees buzzing. He jumped back, aimed a kick at Stan's groin and caught his leg.

"Bastard'n shit," Stan yelled in pain.

Alec was on his feet, fighting restraining hands, his face a red mask of hate to which Kyle launched himself.

And suddenly Nav was there, holding him back, speaking to him. "Calm down, babe, be calm."

A familiar voice cut through the rabble. "What is going on here?" All movement ceased. Jake had that effect. "Someone please explain."

"He attacked me!" Alec yelled.

"Who did?"

Alec shrugged off the hands and stepped forward. "Him, the faggot."

Kyle tensed and felt Nav do the same.

"That language is totally unacceptable here," Jake said with quiet force. He turned to Kyle with one eyebrow raised.

"Yes, I hit him and if he lets me go, I'll finish the job," Kyle challenged.

Alec's answering growl roused him further.

"You have visitors." Jake pointed to where the back door of the main building opened on to the quadrangle. Two uniformed police officers stood watching the proceedings with apparent interest.

"For me?" Kyle blinked.

Jake nodded, and Nav let him go. He glanced at Alec who narrowed his eyes and mouthed something. Conscious of Nav's gentle shove, he reluctantly walked to the police.

"Kyle MacLean?" the tallest one asked. "We've been asked by our Glasgow colleagues to speak to you."

Kyle nodded and followed them through to Jake's office.

"I'm PC Rowan. My neighbour here is PC Armstrong. We're from Stranraer."

As Kyle sat down he felt a wave of tiredness sweep over him as the adrenaline faded from his hyped-up system. He became aware of his throbbing knuckles and cradled his left hand over his right.

"You, okay?" PC Rowan asked in concern. "You don't look so good."

"I'm fine." Kyle realised that his nose was bleeding and accepted a handful of tissues. He shook his head when the man suggested seeing a medic.

"What was going on out there?" the other officer asked. "Did you attack him?"

Uncaring of possible repercussions Kyle nodded. Years of keeping his mouth shut, living by the 'no squeal code', seemed of no consequence when faced with Lola's agony, Ayeesha's shame. "He deserved it. The bastard bullies people for money, rapes women and deals drugs."

Both men looked taken aback.

"What's his name?" PC Rowan asked.

"Alec, don't know his second name."

"Deals drugs, you say?" The other officer frowned. "Anyone else verify that?"

Kyle thought of Lola and shrugged. "Don't know, but a lot of folk will say about the other stuff."

The two men looked at one another and as if in unspoken agreement PC Rowan sat down. "Right you are, Kyle," he said, producing a black notebook from his pocket. "I understand you have some information regarding a Nathan Briggs?"

Kyle nodded and paused to control the rising sadness. "Nathan and I were both in a residential school." Uncertain what to say, he hesitated.

"We've been filled in on your background, son," PC Rowan said kindly.

Dabbing the tissues at his sore nose, Kyle matter-of-factly described their lives in the school and the last time he had seen Nathan.

"A party, you say?" PC Rowan queried.

Reluctant to go into details, Kyle looked down at the floor.

"What kind of party, son?"

Kyle took a deep breath. "A sex party," he blurted. "If Glasgow told you about their investigation, you know what went on."

"Just to be clear, whose party was this?"

Kyle closed his eyes, wishing he'd never agreed to this. "The City Councillor, Bill Fitchett."

PC Rowan scribbled in his notebook. "These parties happened regularly?"

Kyle nodded.

"And this particular one, can you recall the date?"

Kyle reached for memories he'd struggled to forget. "No, but it was the one where the policeman died." The silence was electric. He wished he could swallow the words or the ground could swallow him. When he looked up, PC Rowan was watching him with narrowed eyes, while the other man seemed frozen to the spot.

"Which police officer would that be?"

"Speak to Glasgow," Kyle said in desperation. "Chief Inspector Alex something. She knows all about it." Fear flooded him as it dawned that she probably didn't know. He could only remember discussing it with Aaron and Bee.

"You're claiming that a police officer attended this party?" PC Rowan said slowly. "The one where you saw Nathan for the last time?"

Aware he was blushing, Kyle couldn't meet the man's steady gaze. "I . . . I think so, but maybe I got that wrong. Maybe he wasn't police."

"Do you know his name?"

Kyle almost blurted out 'Cathy', but stopped himself in time. Guilt was choking him. The steady gaze made him want to confess all.

"How did he die?" the second policeman asked from the doorway.

Kyle shrugged. "Dunno, just heard someone had died."

"And you say Glasgow are aware of all this?"

"I think so."

PC Rowan's gaze held him in its grip for a few moments longer, then he abruptly turned away and snapped the notebook shut. "Okay, Kyle. You will need to come to the mainland to sign your statement." He glanced at his colleague. "We'll let you know when. In the meantime, stay away from this Alec."

When he left, he found Navin sitting outside the room, talking to Jake.

"Are you okay?" Navin jumped to his feet.

"I'm fine. You didn't have to wait."

"You missed lunch, but I asked them to keep some food for you."

"He's always looking after your interests." Jake smiled as he stood up. "Tells me Alec attacked you when you were out for a run the other day."

Kyle flicked a look at Navin. "It wasn't really an attack. They were just messing about."

"Ending with you on the floor in a flashback," Jake said.

Uncertain how to respond, Kyle shrugged.

"And Lola saved you?"

Squashing the urge to kick Nav, Kyle said nothing.

"Where is she, by the way? I haven't seen her for a couple of days."

"She . . . she's not well."

"Sorry to hear that. I'll ask the nurse to pop in. You should have that nose checked over too." Jake nodded and headed into his office. "Glad you waited, officers. I think we have a lot to discuss."

"Let's go see about your nose, babe," Navin said, taking Kyle's arm as if to escort him.

Kyle shrugged him off. "I need to see Lola. Tell her there's a nurse coming. And why are you calling me, 'babe', all of a sudden?" he asked as they moved down the corridor. "Quit it."

Chapter Thirty-five

As the circle of chairs began to fill up, Lola had the urge to bolt. She wished she hadn't allowed Kyle to persuade her to come to group, but he was hard to refuse.

"If you stay hiding in your pit like this, you're just letting him win," Kyle had said. "You're over the worst of it now, so come on, show some of that fighting spirit. Nav and I will be beside you."

Although they were, one on each side of her, she still felt afraid. When the nurse had visited, she had immediately spotted the symptoms of withdrawal, but had seemed to accept Lola's explanation that she'd brought the stuff with her. This didn't work with Jake, however, and she'd told him the truth.

"This was your last chance," Jake had said, concerned but resolute. "I accepted you back on the understanding that you had finished with drugs and wanted to work with us on the underlying reasons for your behaviour." She'd lowered her head in shame. "Having said that, I know this time you have been working hard in therapy, and you've established a solid support network."

He paused, and she'd closed her eyes, awaiting the inevitable. "On that basis, I'm prepared to give you a final chance." He'd held up a hand to calm her shock. "I repeat, final chance. I need to see a resumption of your hard work in every area. You will visit the nurse daily for your prescribed medication, and you will stay as far away from Alec as you can. I will deal with him. Is this understood?"

Her agreement had been enthusiastic and heartfelt, but now, sitting with fifteen others all she wanted to do was curl up and cry.

Malcolm, the group therapist, arrived, led by his guide dog, Harry, and took his seat, with smiles and nods as people greeted him. A middle-aged man who'd lost his sight in an accident as a child, Malcolm was popular for his gentle, unassuming manner and ability to help people share their problems.

When the room quietened, Malcolm smiled around the circle of people. Although his eyelids were sealed closed, it always seemed to Lola that warmth beamed out of him.

"Good morning, folks," he said, "It's been a week since we met, so let's begin with updates. Who wants to start?"

"Me," said a girl's voice. "It's Sharon. I will, please."

Malcolm turned in her direction. "Off you go, Sharon."

"I've been here a year." Sharon's eyes were shining with excitement. "And I'm ready to leave. Jake says I can go home soon."

"Can't we all go home if we want?" a man, Lola didn't know, asked.

"Not everyone, Phil. It is Phil, isn't it?"

"Sorry, Malcolm, yes it's me."

Malcolm smiled in his direction. "Some people are here subject to certain mental health or court orders." he said and turned back to Sharon. "Do you want to tell us, Sharon?"

"Sure. I was sent here by the court. I was convicted of theft and shoplifting so many times the jail had a revolving door!" Sharon laughed and people murmured in appreciation. "Then, my social worker persuaded the Sheriff to send me here instead. Working with Bee and here in the group has helped me see that my drinking and taking drugs is all about how my parents neglected me." She sighed. "I've a long way to go yet, but I'll never give up so I can get my boy back." Her voice broke.

"Well done, Sharon," Malcolm said, "You're an example to us all. We should have a party before you leave."

"Barbecue!" someone shouted and others joined in, clapping and stamping their feet.

Within seconds, Sharon was laughing and nodding.

Once the room had quietened down, Lola straightened her shoulders and took a deep breath. "I'll speak next please. It's Lola."

"On you go, Lola."

"I . . . I was scared to speak in the group today, but listening to you, Sharon, you've given me hope," Lola said, trying to keep her voice steady. "As you all know this is my second time here. I blew it last time. Was caught using coke and they chucked me out. I almost blew it again." She stopped, head lowered, ashamed to continue.

Kyle's hand rested against the small of her back. "You're doing fine," he whispered.

She forced the words out. "I . . . I've been using again. Got offered some stuff at a bad time and took it." A pause to fight the urge to run away, then she remembered Kyle's strengthening words when she was ill and raised her head in defiance. The sight of the eyes all focussed on her almost changed her mind, but she carried on. "You know some things about me. I'm a drug addict and my father's rich. He's an actor. If I told you his name you'd know him. What you don't know is . . ." She paused, voice wobbling, then spat the words out. "He started raping me when I was eight years old, got me hooked on drugs when I was twelve years old. Made me have sex with his rich friends in the basement." Her voice ended in a squeak. She squeezed her eyes closed and began to rock back and forward to comfort herself.

Nav's supporting hand joined Kyle's on her back. "You are the bravest woman I have ever met." She heard him say, above the murmuring voices.

"Thank you for your courage, Lola," Malcolm said. "Now, quiet, please. Let's give her space."

Someone handed her a bottle of water, and she took a couple of steadying sips. "When I was fifteen, I ran away from the residential home they'd put me in. I was homeless for months, sleeping rough, living in hostels. I'd do anything for money to get my drugs. The police caught me and took me back, but I ran away again and again." Lola paused. "Then, one day I met this social worker. She was different. Her name was Helen." In her mind's eye she could see her, blond hair in a bun, the most wonderful smile. "She believed in me, and got me into this rehabilitation unit out in the countryside. We had to follow a twelve-step programme, like in AA and NA. I hated it at first." She smiled at the memory. "But it worked. They got me clean, and after that, she got me into another place for women survivors of abuse." She shrugged. "It was a bit strict, I didn't like the rules, so I started going out at night with one of the other girls. Helen was scared I'd relapse, so she referred me here." The next bit was more painful and she took a deep breath. "Two months after I got here, Helen died of a heart attack." Aware of the sad murmurs and the strong hands still on her back, she dipped her head in response. "I began using again and left, but Jake kept in touch. He said, if I stopped, he'd take me back. Gave me something to hold on to."

With a dismissive shake of her head, she looked down at her green toenails. "But I've messed up again, haven't I?" She glanced around at Kyle, whose handsome face reflected concern. "Kyle sorted me out."

His lips twitched in a smile, but his eyes remained troubled.

"I didn't tell you why I started again, did I?"

"I didn't need to know."

"I got a birthday card from my father. That's all." She shrugged. "I was scared. I didn't think he knew where I was. Alec caught me in a bad moment, pretended he cared and that was it."

"Does Jake know?" someone asked.

"Yes, I told him everything, and would you believe he's given me a final, final chance? I'm so grateful, and I'm determined not to blow it this time, but I'll need all the help you guys can give me." She looked around at the circle of faces and felt heartened by the encouraging smiles and comments.

Sharon crossed the room and enveloped her in a huge hug, which made the tears come. "You can do it," Sharon whispered. "If I can do it, anyone can."

"Thank you for sharing, Lola," Malcolm said. "Let us know if there's any additional support we can give you."

"Okay, thanks, Malcolm."

"Does anyone else have news they want to share?"

Lola felt Kyle sit up straighter beside her and remove his supporting hand.

"I have some news," Kyle said. "It's bad news, but I need to share it with you." He paused and took a deep breath. "A friend of mine has been murdered."

Lola joined in the consternation. She glanced at Nav, but he was watching Kyle.

Kyle's eyes were closed, brows drawn. "They chopped his head off, and I know who did it."

The cries of horror roused even the normally placid Harry, who rose and shook himself, scattering golden hairs around the floor. Malcolm placed a steadying hand on the dog's back.

"Careful now, Kyle," he said. "Don't be saying something you regret."

Kyle raised his head. "It's true. It said on the news his body was washed up on Irvine beach a while ago, and now they've found his – his head." He gulped hard. "His name was Nathan. We shared a room in the school."

Harry had settled again and the room was silent.

"I don't know what to say, mate, except I'm sorry for your loss."

Shocked, Lola stared at the speaker.

Stan shrugged and tossed his hair in an almost-feminine gesture.

"Eh . . . thanks," Kyle said.

Stan nodded and looked down at the floor.

Others joined in, offering condolences and words of comfort, and Kyle began to weep.

<>

Meanwhile, in another part of the building, Alec was also in tears. He had struggled through a very difficult interview with Jake, trying to answer questions about his behaviour. None of the usual ploys he adopted had worked with Jake, who repeatedly told him how disappointed he felt. The final, unequivocal decision, that he had to leave the island on the morning ferry, impelled him from the room, with Jake's voice ringing in his ears. "The police and the court have been informed about your drug dealing."

As Alec stumbled into the nearest toilet to hide his emotion, all he could think about was returning home after letting his mother down again, and having to explain to her brother how he'd messed up this time. He looked at his reflection in the mirror above the sink. His eyes were red and fear-filled, but his mouth was twisted with hate. "It's all that wee faggot's fault," he hissed. "Everything was fine until he appeared." Someone came through the door behind him, and he bent over the sink as if washing his hands. When he glanced again in the mirror, his expression looked like panic.

Chapter Thirty-six

When Kyle left Bee's office the following day, Nav was waiting in the corridor. "What's up?"

"Nothing really." Nav said with a good-natured smile. "I was just passing."

Kyle knew he was fibbing, but with a shake of his head, let it go.

"Fancy a walk?" Nav asked and when Kyle nodded, he smiled. "You'll need a jacket. Meet you outside."

They followed the path from the wicket gate at the boundary of the centre's land, into the forest, talking quietly about this and that. Gentle Scottish rain pitter-pattered through the surrounding trees and their footfalls were muffled by the soft forest floor beneath.

With eyes closed, Kyle inhaled deeply. "I love that clean, woody smell."

Nav murmured in agreement then grabbed him when he almost tripped over a tree stump.

"Stupid leg's still not right."

"It's a lot stronger than it was."

"Just like the rest of me." Kyle grinned, squeezing the warm, strong hand still holding his own.

Nav grinned back. "Kyle the Giant-Slayer, eh? How did it go with Bee today?"

Kyle imitated Bee's Canadian accent, "What possessed you to attack Alec?"

"Did you tell her?"

"About the girls? No way." Kyle shrugged. "Well, not in so many words."

"It's all confidential." Nav squeezed his hand and let go.

Kyle looked up at his profile, wondering how to begin. "I – I wanted to talk to you about something," he finally said.

"Okay, fire away."

"The other day, in bed . . . it wasn't you. I . . . I mean, I was half asleep and thought I was back there." Tongue-tied, Kyle sighed.

"It's okay. I sort of worked that out," Nav said with a wry smile. "I got up because I didn't want to make it worse. I . . . I had a hard-on."

Kyle laughed softly. "Me too." Nav looked surprised and for a moment Kyle thought he was going to kiss him. The moment passed, and he was left feeling relieved and a bit disappointed.

It was raining harder, big fat drops permeating the canopy of branches and leaves above.

"Let's find some shelter," Nav said, taking his hand and making for a huge oak standing sentinel in the midst of the pine trees.

Placed around its base were small bundles of fruit and flowers; a chocolate bar, what looked like the remains of a bead necklace, and here and there, a photograph, left there like offerings to a deity. Kyle had heard the story of the magical tree reputed to grant wishes and stepped carefully. When they reached the massive trunk which was warm to the touch, they could hear the rain, but standing beneath the great branches it was quite dry.

"You're shivering," Nav said, hugging him close.

Kyle wasn't, but relaxed into his warmth.

"Tell me about this hard-on." Nav chuckled in his ear.

"How d'you mean?"

"Morning wood, or something else?"

"Not sure," Kyle said, feeling stupid. He felt his face heat and glanced up. Nav was so close, he could smell toothpaste and a hint of coffee, then lips covered his own, soft and hesitant, no demands, or thrusting tongue. He daren't breathe, lest the spell broke. The kiss went on, making him feel languid and warm all-over. Something like an electric shock surged down his body and into his groin, and he heard himself moan into Nav's mouth.

"Okay, babe?" Nav whispered.

Desperate for he didn't know what, Kyle reached up and clumsily pulled Nav's head down. He was trembling as arms enfolded him, lips nuzzled his neck. A hand touched his hair, and he freaked out, struggled to free himself.

"Easy, baby," Nav said, letting him go. "You're okay, you're safe."

"I'm sorry. I don't know what happened, just scared . . ."

"It's ok, you're ok," Nav soothed. "Nothing's going to happen that you don't want to happen. You're in charge, always." With his thumb he brushed away a tear Kyle didn't know he'd shed. "Maybe you're still trying to work out if you're gay or straight, or what you are—"

"No, it's not that." Kyle sniffed and wiped his eyes with the back of one hand. "I know what I am, and it's not about you, either." He looked up at Nav's concerned face. In the muted light his skin took on an olive hue, his features more angular.

Nav smiled, eyes filled with affection. "I understand. Sorry for scaring you. I sometimes forget how young you are."

"Says the man who's all of three years older than me." Kyle chuckled. "You'd think with all my experience," he said turning away and raising his eyes skyward to hide the threatening tears.

Nav caught his shoulder, gently turned him around. "Don't say that, baby." He drew Kyle closer. "There's nothing about you that isn't beautiful and loveable to me." His voice reverberated with emotion, and sincerity shone from his eyes.

Filled with wonder Kyle moved into the encircling safety of his arms.

That night they shared a bed properly for the first time, lying side by side in their tee shirts and boxers. As the days passed, when the light was out, they gradually inched closer until soft kisses became passionate and touches more intimate. In therapy, Kyle had talked, sobbed and screamed his way through numerous memories, but in the dark, touch was the dominant sense. Nav's hand between his legs where many men had touched before, could trigger a bad response and bring forth the monster in his head, with its smells and noises, but these times gradually became less.

True to his word, Nav overstepped no boundaries, and like two virgins they learned from one another. The only drawback was Kyle's inability to tolerate any form of anal penetration, but being in love, they found other ways for both of them to gain satisfaction.

Warm and safe in the dark, listening to Nav's soft post-orgasmic snoring, Kyle reviewed the incredible changes in his life since the fateful day Aaron had run him over. Due to the depravity acted upon him in his earlier life, he had never given much thought to his spirituality or anything remotely supernatural. Evie, he remembered, had called herself 'a woman of faith' and said he too was 'a child of God'. She regularly attended church and had regaled him with stories of modern miracles. At the time, he had dismissed them as stories for the gullible, but now lying curled around Nav's back, breathing him in, amazed at their compatibility, he wondered if there might be something in it after all. Maybe, just maybe, there was someone, somewhere, looking after him.

Chapter Thirty-seven

Bill gazed balefully from his armchair. "I thought you told me this nephew of yours is a loser. So, what's changed?"

"Alec's a tube," Spike agreed, standing before him. "But the description fits; the name's Kyle and he likes to run. We should check it out." He was familiar with Bill's process and waited for him to think it through, controlling a grimace when Bill lit another cigarette.

"Everything I did for that boy," Bill said with a sad sigh, launching into the familiar litany. "I chose him, raised him up, educated him, gave him a life. I trusted him, Spikey."

"I know you did, boss," Spike said in a dutiful voice.

"And he betrayed me," Bill continued in a tone of disbelief. He paused and sat puffing and shaking his head, until his mood abruptly changed. "So, what are you thinking?" he asked through a cloud of smoke which rose to the ceiling to join all the previous clouds, hanging suspended in the airless room.

"Kidnap," Spike explained and described the plan.

"Okay," Bill finally said, "that might work." He blew a column of smoke towards Spike, who covered his mouth and stifled a cough. Bill's mouth twisted into a familiar sneer. "Go and find me the wee grassin' bastard, and do it quick. I've a candidacy meeting with the Party next week."

As Spike left the room, he heard Bill coughing as if his lungs were coming up.

Chapter Thirty-eight

"I need a rest," Navin said, "I'm a bit out of breath."

Kyle slowed and turned around. "But we're only walking."

"You walk fast, it's harder on sand, and it's windy."

Once Nav caught up, Kyle could see he was sweating. He put away his annoyance and smiled. "We've got the cliff to climb yet. Maybe we should leave it until another day?"

They moved to the lee of the cliff where there was grass among the sand and scattered boulders. With a relieved sigh, Navin sat down in a small sheltered area, and Kyle joined him.

"No, I can do it. Just give me ten minutes to get my breath back." Nav stretched out on his back on the warm sand and closed his eyes.

Kyle gazed at him, the shining black hair; long eyelashes, the curve of his cheekbone, light-tan skin, a product of an Indian mother and white Scottish father. Kyle's gaze travelled further as he imagined the body he knew lay beneath the T-shirt and baggy shorts.

"Hey."

Kyle looked up. Nav's eyes were open, glowing with desire. He raised his arms in invitation, and Kyle lay down with him. Kyle's fears about his body's responsiveness preyed on his mind at moments like these. He could climax with Nav's gentle caresses and enthusiastic mouth, and he could give him similar pleasure, but despite Nav's protestations, Kyle knew he yearned for more intimacy. Now, as they kissed and touched each other, something was different. Perhaps due to the absolute privacy, or the salty wind on their skins as they moved against each other. Or perhaps it was Nav's total adoration and desire to give pleasure, but one stroke of his finger where men had plundered before, sent Kyle into orgasmic spasm. Nav's voice joined his in cries of release witnessed only by the wheeling gulls.

When it was over, they laughingly washed each other in a rock pool and lay side by side in the sun to dry.

"That was special," Nav murmured, a flung hand stroking Kyle's shoulder.

Kyle kissed his hand. "Want a drink?" he asked, sitting up to retrieve the water bottle from his backpack.

"You're amazing," Nav said.

"That makes two of us, then."

Nav grinned and sat up. He dusted sand from the hair of his chest and groin. "Gets everywhere, doesn't it?"

Kyle laughed and began to munch a squashed banana from his pack. "There's more fruit in there and a couple of chocolate bars."

"You came prepared," Nav said, going straight for the chocolate.

"Thought we might need some sustenance before the climb." Kyle swallowed some water and stood up to pull on his shorts.

Nav reached out and gently traced his forefinger down Kyle's leg. "You can hardly see the scars now." He leaned forward and kissed the slightly crooked knee. "You're beautiful," he whispered, "Every little bit of you."

"Not so much of the little," Kyle quipped and turned away, shy before the intensity in Nav's eyes. "We don't need to climb up today. We could just walk back along the beach."

"No, let's do it. I feel invigorated." Dressed and smiling, Nav held out a hand.

Half an hour later, Nav was lagging well behind and Kyle sat on a rock to wait for him. "Come on, old man," He laughed at Nav's toiling form. "I thought you were invigorated."

"I've used a lot of energy today," Nav panted, using clumps of grass and heather to haul himself up.

"Me too, but I'm not on my knees. You need to train harder," Kyle said, then relented and held out his hand. "Here, grab on."

Nav reached for his outstretched hand and looked up with his open, trusting smile, white teeth flashing in the sunshine. Their hands met. His gaze shifted upwards, and his expression changed. "Who's that? What's going on?"

Kyle turned his head.

"Hi there," Spike said.

PART THREE

Chapter Thirty-nine

"Where to, Spike?"

"Head straight for the ferry terminal. We'll change cars on the way." Spike looked over his shoulder at Kyle, lying in drug-induced sleep beneath the blanket on the back seat.

"D'you think the Paki's dead?"

"Who knows?" Spike shrugged.

"Maybe I shouldn't have hit him so hard."

"Stop worrying about it, Paul. No-one knows we're here, and we'll be off the island again soon." As they reached the end of the dirt track and drove on to the main road, Spike thought of the surprisingly easy collection. For once, Alec's information had proved accurate. Kyle ran along the same route every day, so all they had to do was wait at the top of the cliff-path.

Kyle moaned and shifted.

"Pull over," Spike said. By the time he'd climbed in the back, Kyle was again motionless. Nevertheless, Spike checked his pulse, breathing and lifted his eyelids. "He seems fine." He moved back to the passenger seat and checked the map. "The turn-off is about two miles before the ferry port."

When they opened the doors of the dilapidated barn Paul burst out laughing at the sight of the shining, black hearse. "What a fucking great idea!"

"Keys are in the ignition. Bring it out and help me get the boy into the coffin."

"Won't he suffocate?" Paul asked, once they'd settled Kyle into the plush interior and closed the lid.

"It has airholes, idiot. Bill uses them to bring in special orders. Put on the chauffeur outfit and let's go." Spike exchanged his own clothes and prepared to look suitably solemn as they joined the short ferry queue.

They were waved through without a hitch by respectful-looking crew members, with the only concern being the automatic camera-flash at disembarkation.

As they set off on the road north, Spike glanced back at the flower-bedecked coffin. He was aware of a moment of nostalgia. Although some boys pretended defiance to titillate the customers, Kyle never did. His was real, no matter the level of punishment. It had earned him a twisted sort of respect from some of Bill's customers and even Bill himself. Given the boy's potential, it saddened Spike that he was taking him to almost certain death.

"Can I switch on the radio?" Paul interrupted his thoughts.

"Keep it low and watch your speed. Remember, cameras."

Chapter Forty

Kyle came to with slow, arduous gasps. It was pitch dark. His head thumped, and the air was stale with his own body odour. He felt clamped in a vice. He strained and struggled until he freed an arm from elbow to hand. Above him, his fingers touched wood. He scraped his nails back and forward. *A box. I'm in a box.* With an effort, he freed his other arm and pushed up with both hands. Nothing moved. Panic consumed him. He choked out a scream, sickness in his mouth. Sudden brightness blinded him, until all he could see was Bill.

"Well, well, here we are at last." Bill's smile didn't reach his eyes. "You've been hard to track down, boy."

Kyle retched again, and his bladder almost emptied itself. "I need a pee."

With a bark of laughter, Bill stepped back. "Take him to the bog, Spike, and hose him down. He stinks."

Afterwards, naked and shivering, he was hauled into what looked like a barn or warehouse and strapped to a chair, his hands to the chair-arms and his ankles to the legs.

"What's he going to do, Spike?" he begged.

Spike gazed at him with what looked like regret. "You brought this on yourself," he said. "Just tell him the truth, and it'll be over quickly." He walked away.

With the removal of his presence, Kyle felt alone and even more afraid. A man he didn't know placed a round table, like Aaron had in the garden, next to him. It had a hole in the middle, presumably for an umbrella, and was encrusted with dirt and something that could have been blood. A second one carried over a tray, laid it down gently and smiled. Following his gaze, Kyle panicked. Whips and handcuffs he could cope with, even nipple-clamps, if they weren't too tight. He'd been beaten and tied up, suspended from a net while men in masks took turns, but the implements arrayed on the tray weren't meant for games.

He froze as Bill appeared and lifted the pliers, testing their flexibility.

"Please, Bill, you don't need to do this."

"Don't I?" Bill leaned close to him and sniffed, nostrils flaring. "Ah, I love the smell of fear."

<>

"We've got them, Detective Inspector!" The young PC yelled as he flung her office door open. "It's a hearse, they're in a hearse."

"Well done, Michael." She rose from her desk and followed him to the small group gathered around the computer monitor.

The seated officer nodded at her and replayed the CCTV video, showing the ship docking at the Stranraer ferry terminal. The only vehicle to leave, a hearse, made its slow way towards the gate and on to the main road. "They were told to hold all disembarking vehicles, Inspector."

"But decided that didn't include a hearse?" she finished.

He nodded and rolled his eyes. "But the good news is that they sent us a photo of the driver and passenger. Both are associates of Bill Fitchett."

She smiled in satisfaction. "Inform the locals and arrange air support."

<>

Kyle's broken fingers and torn-out nails screamed desperate messages to his overloaded brain and escaped as animal-howls through gritted teeth. He felt a plastic bottle against his mouth and choked on water as he rocked back and forth in his agony.

"I don't enjoy this, you know," Bill said, "especially with boys like you. We've known each other a long time, haven't we?" He stroked a hand across Kyle's cheek making him flinch. Bill's voice changed to a jovial tone. "I remember when you first came to us. You were a cute wee bastard with your freckled face and glasses."

"Please, please, no more."

"Well, didn't you? Didn't you have glasses like the Milky Bar kid?"

"Yes," Kyle groaned, although he knew he hadn't. Bill squeezed his nipple with pliers again. He screamed, and the pungent smell of urine filled his nostrils.

"Tell me again what happened to Cathy."

"I've told you, please, I've told you."

"Tell me again."

It was a nightmare. Kyle repeated the scenario from beginning to end, uncertain if his words were in sequence, or even if they made sense anymore. When he finished, he peered upwards.

Bill stared through narrowed eyelids. "So, you did kill her?"

"What? No." Kyle gasped in horror. "It was an accident."

"But you've just told me that you kneed her in the bollocks, and she went down."

"No, I mean yes, but she tripped and . . . and fell back."

The punch in his left eye took him by surprise. He reeled against the restraints, conscious only of lightning flashes of pain.

"That's for lying to me."

<>

Aaron looked down at the young man on the trolley. Although he seemed to be asleep, Navin's brows were drawn as if in pain. Not wishing to disturb him, Aaron prepared to leave.

"Wait, who are you?"

"Hi, Navin. I'm Aaron, Kyle's friend."

Navin's huge, dark eyes opened wide. "Have they found him? Is he safe?" He tried to sit up.

"Take it easy, son." Aaron gently pushed him back down. "Not yet."

"Oh, God please help him" Navin said, eyes filling with tears.

Almost weeping too, Aaron patted his shoulder. "Can you tell me what happened?"

"It's a bit blurry." Navin shook his head as if to clear it. "We were climbing up towards the road, Kyle was in front. There was a man *at the* top, leaning over. He said, hello or something, then I think I was hit." He rubbed his eyes. "I . . . I told the police, I don't know what happened next. Jake and Bee found me on the road. I don't know how I got there."

Aaron felt a great lump form in his gut. "What did the man look like?" He waited a moment as Navin thought back.

"He was white, with white hair." Navin broke down. "It's my fault. I made Ky climb up . . . showing off."

All Aaron's instincts were screaming alert, but before he could react, the cubical curtain opened, and Dave appeared.

"Stuart phoned. Sandi's in hospital."

<>

With a gasp of shock Kyle came to. His head hung low, and his throbbing left eye dripped blood.

"Welcome back." Bill loomed, an empty water bottle in his hand. "Now let's stop playing games, boy. We've established that you killed Cathy."

Kyle raised his head. "Accident," he whispered and flinched at the threatening fist.

"If it was an accident," Spike said from behind him, "why did you run away?" He moved into Kyle's line of sight. "Why didn't you phone me?"

Kyle had no answer other than the truth. "I wanted to . . . to escape. Sean just went along with it."

"And died for it."

Defeated, Kyle wept.

"Escape?" Bill asked. "Escape what?"

Head hanging, trying not to be sick, Kyle shook his head.

"I think he means us," Spike said.

"You ungrateful wee cunt," Bill swore, eyes wide in outrage. "Everything I've done for you. Took you out of the mire, gave you a home and a good job. Made sure you only did special parties." He gazed at Spike in indignation and disbelief.

"No gratitude," Spike commented.

"I trusted you," Bill ranted. "Let you work in my office, didn't I? Gave you new clothes and things, didn't I?" He grabbed Kyle's chin. "Didn't I?"

"Yes," Kyle mumbled.

"I wasn't bad to you, was I?"

Presumably taking Kyle's groan as affirmation, Bill sat in a chair opposite him and lit a cigarette. "What's to escape from?" he said to Spike in a hurt tone. "You'd think we were monsters or something. He puffed on his cigarette. "This boy and me have had some good times together, like you and me did."

Spike made no reply.

Unable to tear his gaze from the lumpy, hairy belly bulging through Bill's straining shirt, Kyle had an unwanted memory of bouncing drunkenly on that fat stomach to the accompaniment of Bill's roar of 'Ride'em, cowboy.' Sobbing helplessly, he glimpsed the black legs of the spider tattoo which terrified him as a child, remembering how it seemed to crawl and leap at him with each of Bill's movements.

"I think he's had enough for now, boss," Spike said.

Bill stood up. "Not yet. I haven't finished."

"Please, no more," Kyle begged.

"Tell me the truth." Bill leaned over and stubbed out his cigarette on Kyle's broken hand, making him scream. "Tell me again. What was on the pen drive you gave the police?"

"I told you, just . . . just some minutes."

Bill sighed in irritation. "What minutes?"

"I can't remember. Please, it's too long ago." Kyle wept and almost screamed again when Bill lifted a set of bolt cutters.

Bill's lips were drawn back from his clenched teeth as he gripped Kyle's left pinky making him cry out. "Try harder, boy, or I'll rip it off." He tightened his grip. "Then, finger number two."

In that agonising moment, Kyle knew without a shred of doubt that he was going to die. With the knowledge came a familiar sense of calm. He wasn't afraid of dying, had come to terms with pain and death long ago. All it would have taken was one of his 'customers' to slip up and go too far, and he'd thought about suicide often enough, but not like this, not for this bastard's pleasure. Excruciating pain pulsed through every part of him, but dragging up strength he did not know he possessed, he yelled his defiance.

Bill's expression changed, eyes widening.

"I was saving it for months," Kyle screamed. "The pen-drive was full. They know all about you, you fucking monster. They should strangle you slowly." Shocked at himself, Kyle watched in terror as Bill's mouth twisted into a rictus of hate.

"Boss," a voice shouted. "The cops are here."

Bill froze.

Petrified, Kyle stared. He knew every line, every nasal hair, every blackhead.

The roaring sound of a hovering helicopter drowned all.

Bill sneered as the jaws of the cutters came together snipping off Kyle's finger. He was holding it up in triumph as Kyle slid into a welcoming darkness.

Chapter Forty-one

Aaron pushed through the swing doors into the surgical ward. His stomach churned with anticipation and, if he was honest, fear of what he would find. Already feeling anxious from visiting Sandi lying pale and exhausted and worried about his new son's health, he paused to show his ID to the policeman guarding Kyle's room.

"Don't look so worried," the escorting staff nurse whispered, patting his shoulder.

"What did they do to him?"

The woman took a deep breath. "He's been hit several times on the face probably with a closed fist, seriously damaging his left eye which might have to be removed. His stomach is badly bruised and it looks like someone had a go with something on a nipple." He swallowed hard and she paused in sympathy. "They broke two of his fingers, ripped out the nails and severed his left little finger. By the time the medics got there, it was nowhere to be found, so of course it couldn't be reattached, and he's lost a lot of blood."

Aaron inhaled deeply to combat the sudden wave of dizziness.

"Are you okay?" she asked, holding his elbow. "This level of violence is always a terrible shock, but he will recover. He's young and strong."

Aaron nodded. "Physically anyway," he murmured.

"If you're sure you're alright, I'll leave you to it."

"I'm fine, thanks."

Kyle was scarcely recognisable. His left eye was heavily bandaged, and his swollen face a mass of bruises and cuts. The edge of a dressing could be seen poking out from his hospital top. He had an IV attached to his right hand, and his left, heavily bandaged, was suspended above him.

In Aaron's line of work, apart from those who attempted suicide, physically traumatised patients were less than frequent, and the sight of someone he cared about in such a state, made him want to howl in anguish. He struggled to distance himself as he had to in his working life to avoid sliding into the pit of pain with the patient, but only partially succeeded.

"Hey there," he whispered, then wished he'd stayed silent when Kyle jerked and opened one eye.

Shock quickly shifted to recognition. "Aaron," Kyle croaked and began to hiccup great helpless sobs.

Desperate to comfort him, but afraid to hurt, Aaron finally settled on cupping each shoulder in a gentle grip. Hardly aware of what he was doing, he bent forward and kissed the drawn brow, then wished he hadn't when it seemed to make Kyle even more distressed.

After a while, Kyle gradually calmed. Aaron gently patted his face dry with a tissue and helped him blow his nose. "Do you need anything? Drink of water?"

Kyle nodded, sucked from the straw and lay back as if he'd made a great effort. Lifting over the visitor's chair, Aaron sat beside him and waited until he'd recovered his strength.

After a few minutes, Kyle opened his good eye and attempted a crooked smile. "Where am I?"

"You're in Glasgow."

"How did I get here?"

Aaron smiled. "Nothing's too good for you – you travelled in style by helicopter. How are you feeling?"

"Not sure," Kyle said with an attempt at a shrug which made him wince, then his expression changed. "Nav?"

Aaron nodded and smiled. "He's fine, I visited him in Stranraer Hospital. He has concussion. He was punched and hit his head. Dave's bringing him up later today. He can stay in your old room."

"Thanks." Kyle's eyelid drooped, but he blinked himself awake. His voice strengthened, and he asked the inevitable question. "Did they get him?"

"Yes." Aaron watched an expression of relief cross the once bright, beautiful face. "He tried to escape in a car, but the helicopter followed him. He was taken into custody, protesting loudly, I believe, with four other men. Spike wasn't one of them."

Kyle's good eye was closing. "Spike didn't hurt me," he whispered. A moment later, he was snoring.

Aaron checked his neck pulse and lightly stroked his fingers across his brow, thinking of what this brave young man had endured through his life. The sorrow of it. The great, crushing outrage of it.

After a while, lulled by gentle snores, he drifted and came to with a start to the sound of weeping. Navin was bent over Kyle, kissing his brow. For a moment, Aaron thought something awful had happened, then he heard the whispered endearments and knew it was time to leave.

Dave was waiting outside the door. "How're you doing?" He greeted Aaron with a rueful smile.

"Shouldn't that be how's *he* doing?" Aaron quipped as they walked side-by-side along the corridor. He glanced at Dave. The honesty in his world-weary gaze was too much, and he looked away.

"Stuart's been keeping me informed about everything and everybody, as usual."

"He's in the wrong job, should be a newspaper reporter. Do you want a coffee?"

Dave nodded in agreement and followed him to the nearest hospital snack-bar where Aaron ordered, while he found a quiet table.

"What's happening with Fitchett?" Aaron asked once they'd settled.

"His lawyers are demanding bail. The Fiscal is opposing it, and the hunt's on for Spike."

"Kyle says that Spike didn't hurt him."

Dave stirred sugar into his coffee. "That'll be in his favour, once he's caught. The police will want to interview Kyle as soon as. How do you think he's doing?"

"He's in a bad way and lost a lot of blood," Aaron said taking a sip of coffee, "but he's tough and very resilient. He'll do everything he can to bring the bastard down."

Dave nodded in agreement. "I'll get in to see him before I go home. Stu tells me your children are born."

Warmth filled Aaron's chest and he found himself grinning. "A beautiful boy and girl. The girl has the look of Evie. The boy has blond hair, like Sandi. He was born first." He paused and saddened. "Although he isn't well, breathing difficulties. We're hoping it's not his heart."

"I'm sorry to hear that. And the girl?"

Aaron smiled. "Clancy, her name's Clancy, and he's Ollie, short for Oliver. She's just a bundle of energy and already putting on weight. Wish she could share some with her brother."

"Be thankful she's okay. I'd love to meet them. Stuart and I bought them some gifts."

"Sure, I'll arrange it with Sandi."

"How is she?"

"Tired, but she's tough and resilient too."

Dave's eyes searched his own.

"We're not getting on any better," Aaron admitted. "In fact it was getting worse the more her pregnancy progressed. At the end, there she could hardly stand me to be in the same room." He sat back in his chair and glanced around the café. One table in the corner made him smile in spite of himself, surrounded as it was by four legless men in wheelchairs tucking in to bacon rolls with obvious gusto.

"They're making up for hospital food," Dave commented, following his gaze. "How come you weren't there at the birth?"

Aaron shrugged. "I ought to have been, I know, but when I heard Kyle was missing, there was no choice, to be honest with you."

He smiled ruefully. "It's no excuse, but she wasn't due for another two weeks."

"And I'm the last person to judge you." Dave's eyes were filled with compassion. "Just try to remember how old he is."

Aaron smiled sadly and shook his head. "I don't expect anything from him. He has Navin and a whole new life to live, which I won't be a big part of, but when he was missing, and seeing him all broken like that, it made me realise - face the truth - it's brought everything to a head," he said looking at Dave. "I can't stay with Sandi any longer. It's over." He paused and fiddled with his coffee cup, feeling the hurt of the statement.

"Does she feel the same?"

"I don't know what she feels, other than dislike."

"Not that I have a lot of experience," Dave said choosing his words, "but I've heard that women can be quite awkward during pregnancy."

Aaron chuckled. "That's true, it's the hormones, but I think it's been a bit more than that with Sandi."

They sat in silence for a few moments, each absorbed in his own thoughts.

"What are you going to do?" Dave finally asked.

"Leave. I'll wait until we're clearer about Ollie's health, but I'm leaving. She can have the house for as long as she needs and I'll support her and the twins in every way I can. They're my responsibility. I'm not abandoning them."

"Where will you go?"

"Stay in the hospital for a bit." Aaron shrugged. "Haven't spoken to Stu about it yet, but maybe get a short-term let on a flat or something until the house is sold. There are often flats to rent on the notice-board at work." He paused and wiped his mouth with a napkin. "I've taken paternity leave, so I'll hunt one up. Navin can come with us, and once Kyle's out of hospital they can both stay, if they want."

As they stood up, Dave gave Aaron's shoulder an affectionate squeeze. "I'm sorry you're going through this. A break-up is always hellish, especially if there are kids involved, but I'm glad you've finally made the decision."

"Me too," Aaron said as they left the snack-bar. "I just hope Sandi will see it that way."

Chapter Forty-two

"You had to wait until I was at my weakest, Aaron. You cruel bastard," Sandi snarled.

Tormented with guilt, Aaron dismissed the thought that she looked anything but weak and tried to sound reasonable. "It's been six weeks, Sandi. You're a lot stronger now—"

"How would you know?" she interrupted, getting up from the table and yanking open the dishwasher. "You're never here." None-too-gently, she began filling the machine with breakfast dishes. "Got to visit Evie," she said in a sneering imitation of his voice. "Can't take you shopping today – promised to take Kyle out." She spat the last two words.

"Twice," Aaron said, rising to the bait in-spite-of himself. "I've taken him out twice since the children were born, and surely you don't begrudge me seeing my sister?" He grabbed his half-full coffee mug before she snatched it away and took a deep breath to calm himself.

"Why now?" She slammed the machine door shut and turned around to face him. "Why couldn't you at least wait until Ollie comes home to tell me you're leaving?"

Despite all, the raw pain in her voice made him want to weep. "Sandi—"

"Don't you dare say it will never happen. You heard what the doctor said, where there's life, there's hope."

"Ollie isn't well." Aaron said quietly, "He's very ill, and until the ultrasound, we can't be sure if it's his heart or—"

"I know that." she snapped. "I'm his mother. I sit with him for hours while you're doing who knows what."

"Looking after Clancy." Aaron interjected.

"It's all your fault, anyway." Sandi continued as if he hadn't spoken. "If you'd been here when you were needed, instead of chasing after your latest boy-tart, my son wouldn't be dying now." It was the usual litany, stirring his guilt.

"I've explained all that, Sandi," he said in a reasonable tone. "There was no indication that you'd start early. I made sure you had your mother with you before I left, and as it turned out, you had a normal birth. The doctors have confirmed that Ollie's illness has nothing to do with his birth." He stopped as he took in her body language. Her head was lowered, her body shaking, and her hands were in tight fists. "Sandi?"

Very slowly she raised her head. Her face was red and wet with tears.

He rose and took a step towards her, hand outstretched to comfort.

"Don't touch me, you bastard, you absolute bastard."

Her tone was so vicious that he stepped back. For an instant her eyes held a strange, unfocussed expression, which concerned him. Clancy's waking cry drew his immediate attention, and he headed for her room.

Clancy lay in her pink and white cot, arms and legs waving. Her little face was screwed up; her mouth wide with screams which became gurgles the moment Aaron cradled her in his arms. Although he knew it wasn't possible, he felt his heart swell with love. "Good morning, little one," he whispered.

"Hand her over." Sandi stood in the nursery doorway.

"She's fine here. I'll change her and bring her through for you to feed her."

"Give me my baby."

"Calm down, Sandi. She's my baby too."

"No, she isn't."

His breath caught. It was finally here. What he had dreaded for months. Instinctively, he held Clancy closer and stared in silence. The pulsing pain in his throat was unbearable.

Sandi's lovely eyes were narrowed, the mouth he had found so sexy, twisted in a parody of a smile. "That shocked you, didn't it? Mr Oh-So-Clever Douglas. How could you think my beautiful children could have anything to do with you?"

Aaron found his voice. "What are you saying?"

"I'm saying," she spat, "they're not yours. You're not man enough to father children."

"Please don't say this because you're angry with me."

She looked at him with an expression he had never seen before. It was as if she hated him.

"Words of one syllable. They. Are. Not. Yours. Their father is a man, not a thing like you."

"Who?" he croaked out.

"You'll never know." She reached out her arms. "Give me my daughter."

Horrified but helpless to resist, he kissed Clancy before he handed her over. "Why, Sandi?" he said hoarsely.

"Why? Why?" She almost screamed, eyes so wide her pupils looked ready to pop. "Why do you think?" Clancy began to cry, and she rocked her and lowered her voice. "Isn't it obvious? I can't compete with a man."

"But, there is no man."

"If it was a woman, I'd know what to do, but—"

Aaron raised his voice. "There is no man."

"There's always a man," she yelled making Clancy cry again.

"Calm down. You're frightening her," he said, concerned for the baby's safety.

"There always has been," she ranted, ignoring him. "And he's still here."

His confusion cleared, replaced by disbelief. "You mean, Stuart? But Stuart's with—"

"Yes, I know," she spat, rocking Clancy against her. "But he's still here, isn't he? He's here more often than with his so-called husband."

Aaron couldn't believe what he was hearing, and she saw it in his eyes. His silence seemed to wind her up again.

"Get out, just get out," she yelled, and for Clancy's sake he complied. "And don't come back," she shouted after him.

With no plan in mind he grabbed a jacket, stamped into his boots and headed for the woodland where Dave exercised his dogs when he visited. As he walked through the trees, he replayed what had just happened, her voice screeching over and over, 'They're not yours. You're not man enough,' until he vomited his breakfast on the path. Trembling, he sat on a log and covered his face with his hands.

One part of his brain recognised that he was in shock. The other could not comprehend what had just happened. *I'm a fool,* he thought, *arrogant fool.*

As he had fried the bacon, he had actually practiced his speech to her, prepared for her tears, prepared to comfort her, little knowing that she had her own, much bigger bombshell to drop. The pain came like a wave through his belly and into his chest. He saw again the little face, her big dark eyes so like his own, like Evie's. He paused. Ollie also had those eyes, although his hair was blonder, like Sandi's. They were twins, like him and Evie. Sandi had no twins in her family. When his mobile rang he almost didn't answer, but it was Evie in that mysterious way of communicating they had between them.

"What's happened?" she asked.

So, he told her and waited while she poured her shock and rage into his ear. "Hang on, sis. I'd said I was leaving."

"That's nothing to do with it. The bitch betrayed you with some soldier and wasn't going to tell you. She'd have let you bring up another man's children."

"We don't know that—"

"Of course we do," Evie railed. "You're too soft, that's your trouble. My God, I've known her all my life, wait 'til I get my hands on her. You have rights, you're married . . . "

As she ranted on, Aaron's mood began to lift, and he didn't feel quite so bereft. "I do have rights, don't I?"

"Of course you do. She can't just say they're not yours, and that's it. They are legally yours, no matter how many men she's rolled around with in the jungle."

In spite of himself, Aaron snorted a laugh. "It's not jungle and knowing Sandi, she wouldn't roll around with anyone."

"Well, she clearly did with someone. Ok, this is what to do," Evie got into her stride, "You go home and pack. You tell her you want a DNA test. You come and stay with me, or better still you stay there in case she tries to take the children out of the country. I'll tell Cameron he has a new client."

"Slow down, sis, one step at a time. I don't know about moving out yet, but when I do you'll be the first to know. Tell Cameron I'd be delighted for him to legally represent me, if he has the time. I'm going to go now. We have an appointment with Ollie's doctor."

Back at home, he found Clancy, fully dressed, cooing happily at the hanging lights and rattles above her cot. He lifted her and cuddled her close.

"I've phoned a taxi," Sandi said from the doorway.

"Cancel it. We're going in the car."

Before they set off, he turned to her. She'd been crying, and it gave him momentary pause. "We're married, Sandi. The twins are legally mine." Her brow raised and she blinked a few times. "I'm having a DNA test."

"I won't let you."

"You can't stop me."

She turned her head to face the passenger window and said nothing.

"I know I've hurt you at a difficult time," he began.

"Fuck off."

He waited a moment, put the car into gear and drove on towards the motorway.

"I'm moving out today," she finally said. "I'm going to stay with Mum, and Clancy comes with me."

"There's no need for that. It's Clancy's home. I'll move."

"Aren't you forgetting Ollie?"

"Of course not. It's his home too."

She started crying. "Why are you such a bastard?"

Aaron couldn't find the words to express what he was feeling. They drove on in silence, punctuated by her sobs.

Chapter Forty-three

The consultant's face was grave as he gave them the news. Although expecting it, Aaron's stomach dipped and a sudden rush of tears threatened to choke him. Sandi seemed to be almost fainting, so he supported her with one arm and held Clancy with the other.

"I know it doesn't help, Mrs and Mrs Douglas, but I am so sorry." The consultant looked around his mid-forties, with brown hair beginning to recede and blue eyes full of compassion. Clancy gurgled her own response, and Aaron kissed her head.

"It also doesn't help at the moment, I'm sure, but you have a beautiful, healthy daughter."

"No, it doesn't," Sandi sobbed as she leaned against Aaron.

"What happens next, if we agree?" Aaron asked.

With an obvious effort, the man became all professional. He straightened in his chair and consulted the file before him on the desk.

"As you know, your son is receiving pain medication which will continue, but life-support would stop."

Sandi emitted a muffled howl, and Aaron pulled her closer. "Easy, sweetheart. We knew this was coming." Her head shook in denial against his chest. "How long?"

"I can't be accurate, but if we stop today, a matter of hours."

"Can we stay with him?"

"Of course. You'll have a private room."

By mutual consent, they each called their closest family members, Sandi's mother and Aaron's sister. After emotional goodbyes had been said, they left with Clancy, while her tiny brother remained with his grieving parents.

At 4am, Aaron jerked awake, his gaze searching the warm, dimly-lit room. Opposite him, Sandi lay on a day-bed covered by a blanket. Her eyes were closed, and she cradled her baby against her breast. Aaron stared at the pale, little face and crossed the room to check his breathing.

"Don't touch him," Sandi said.

"I'm just checking." Before he even reached him, Aaron knew his son was gone.

"Don't touch him," Sandi warned, pulling the stiff little body closer.

Filled with sorrow, Aaron knelt beside them. "It's ok," he whispered. "It's ok."

Chapter Forty-four

Bill was grinning maniacally, like the ventriloquist's dummy from the horror film. The bolt-cutters seemed huge between his fingers as he aimed for Kyle's eye and plunged.

Kyle's scream brought Nav rushing from the kitchen, the door swinging in his wake. He wore an apron with a picture of a tin of beans and a tin-opener, and as he flung himself to his knees before Kyle, it got trapped, propelling him almost into Kyle's lap.

They apologised in unison and ended up holding each other's hands. "No, I'm sorry," Kyle repeated, avoiding touching his eyepatch to check it had been a dream. "Are you okay?"

"I'm fine," Nav said. His face was thinner than it used to be, and his brow always seemed to be drawn. "Another bad dream. You need to tell the doctor."

Kyle shook his head. "It'll pass."

"It's been almost two months, and you're still post-traumatic stressing."

Nav leaned up and kissed him lightly.

"*I* am?" Kyle laughed, kissing him back. "You shot through here like a bullet out of a gun. What're you cooking, anyway?"

"Ah, that would be telling." Nav grinned and tapped the side of his nose.

"Well, I can smell spices, so, is it curry?"

"That's for me to know, and you to guess when you eat it." With a knowing wink, Nav sat back on his heels and pulled off the apron. "How's your finger?"

"Okay, but the new one's taking it's time to grow," Kyle smiled.

"Glad it's only your finger." Nav slid a hand down from chest to groin and gently squeezed, grinning at Kyle's reaction.

"C'mere, you," Kyle said roughly, drawing him up between his legs and kissing him hard.

 Nav groaned and opened his mouth to him.

"Let's switch off the curry," Kyle whispered.

"Already done," Nav whispered back, unzipping him.

Kyle gasped and clutched the chair-arms as the warm hand stroked him, and the hot mouth took him in. His eager, young body reached a fast, shuddering orgasm and he lay panting as Nav began to bring himself off. "Let me," Kyle said, reaching for him.

Afterwards, Nav stroked a knuckle down his cheek, his gaze adoring. "I love making love to you," he whispered. "You're so sexy when you come for me."

Kyle grabbed the knuckle and kissed it. "Still wish we could fuck?"

"We will, babe. I guarantee it."

They ate in the tiny kitchen, Kyle downing cold water and piling on yoghurt to assuage the heat of the food. "This is amazing," he said between mouthfuls, "Nippy, but it has a great taste."

"Family recipe. My mum used to make it."

"Do you have family in India?"

Navin nodded. "I've never been. My mum was born here, but her parents left their family behind when they emigrated."

"Wouldn't you like to find them?" Kyle asked as the phone rang in the living room and Nav went to answer it. He came back with a face like thunder. "What's up?"

"They've found you again. That was the *Daily Tribune* looking for an interview. I told them to piss off."

Kyle sighed and wiped his mouth with a paper towel. "Sometimes, I wish we'd stayed in Aaron's. I know we moved for privacy," he continued before Nav could speak, "and it's good, but it seems to be easier to find me."

"We agreed they'd find you wherever you are." Navin paused, eyebrows raised, "Time for the Indian trip?"

The surge of excitement took Kyle by surprise. They looked at one another, then he came back down to earth. "I have to stay for the trial."

"Afterwards?" Nav said, hesitating. "Honeymoon?"

Kyle almost choked on a mouthful of water.

Nav looked nervous, dark eyes filled with questions.

"Are you proposing to me, handsome?" Kyle finally got out.

Taking a deep breath, Nav reached across the remains of the meal and took his hand. "Will you marry me?" he asked in a trembling tone.

Kyle held the hand between both of his, raised it up and kissed the palm. "Try and stop me," he replied.

<>

Their joy was dampened when Aaron phoned with sad news.

"Ollie's gone," he said, "We agreed to them switching off life-support." His voice trembled. "He just slipped away in the early hours yesterday."

"God, Aaron, I'm so sorry," Kyle said, switching on the phone speaker.

"Me too," Nav said.

"Thanks, it's for the best. There was no betterment."

Kyle could hear the pain in his voice and wanted to help somehow. "How are you? Are you at home? Can we come over?"

"Thanks, but not now. Sandi's here." Aaron's tone changed. "How are you doing?"

"I'm fine.

"He's not." Nav butted in, making Kyle roll his eyes with annoyance. "He's still having bad dreams and the newspapers have found him again."

"He doesn't need to hear that, Nav."

"That's okay," Aaron said. "Gives me something else to think about. Why don't you go back to the island, finish your programme?

Nav was nodding hard and repeatedly mouthing, "Yes."

"I'll think about it," Kyle said.

"Do that," Aaron said, "and Dave said to tell you that three teachers and two more ex-residents have now given statements."

"Yes, Alison my liaison told me," Kyle said, as Nav cleared away. "She says it's going to be a huge case, with trials running simultaneously in London and Glasgow. Anyway, I won't keep you, Aaron. I'm so sorry again about Ollie. Once things have – well when you're ready, we can meet for a drink or something."

"Okay. I'll let you know when the funeral is."

After they said goodbye, Nav brought two cups of coffee to the table. "You didn't tell him? About us?"

"Didn't seem appropriate." Kyle shrugged.

Chapter Forty-five

In the third row of pews, Kyle sat next to Nav with Stuart at one side and Dave, looking quite different in a dark suit and hair tied back with a black ribbon, at the other.

To Kyle's surprise, it was a Catholic funeral, not that he'd had much experience of funerals, but Aaron's religion had never occurred to him. He stood up when everyone else did and watched in confused fascination how people responded to the priest's words. When it came to blessing the tiny coffin, which Aaron had carried in, face wet with tears, Kyle felt moved by the way he and Sandi hung on to each other, united in grief. Hidden beneath their folded coats, Nav's hand crept into his own while they listened to the readings from the pulpit.

Afterwards in the church hall, they made an effort to eat some of the buffet and talk to people they didn't know.

"You two look lost," Dave commented, joining them with his plate of food.

Kyle turned to him in relief. "When can we leave?"

"Anytime you like. What time is the boat?"

"Four o'clock, but we wanted to get changed in your place first, remember."

"Uh-huh." Dave nodded. "Why don't you say your goodbyes while I round-up Stuart?"

<>

As he watched the land recede, Kyle recalled his first journey to the island and smiled, remembering how Stuart had fallen into the sea and had to be rescued. How he himself had wanted to jump off the ship and swim back to shore. He had been so anxious and more than a little bit scared of Lola. It was like a lifetime ago.

Nav called his name, and he joined him on a bench, with Bryn, the ex-soldier Dave had hired to protect them.

"How does it feel, going back?" Bryn asked, accepting a coffee from Nav.

Dave had assured them that the capable-looking young man knew what he was about and would defend them both with his life, if necessary. Kyle didn't believe he needed protection anymore, but had nevertheless been reassured at the sight of the shoulder holster under Bryn's jacket.

"Bit like going home, in a way."

"Even after what happened there?"

Kyle considered the question. "Can't remember much about it," he mused. "Last thing I do remember was Spike with a hypodermic." A coldness washed through him, making him shudder.

"He's the bastard's right-hand man?'

"Uh-huh."

"Where is he now?"

"On the run," Nav said, taking a swallow of coffee and immediately screwing up his face. "That's disgusting." He stood to throw it overboard.

"Give it here," Bryn said, "It's hot and wet. D'you think he might turn up here?"

Kyle shook his head.

"He hurt you pretty bad," Bryn said, eyeing Kyle's scarred hand and eye-patch.

"That wasn't him. Bill likes to do his own torture. He cut off my finger with a pair of bolt cutters." Kyle spoke calmly, but felt his stomach jerk at the memory.

"Bloody hell," Bryn exclaimed. "He's a bad bastard, right enough."

Kyle stood up and moved to the rail. With a huff of effort, he threw his half-full cup over the side and watched how the wind caught it and whirled it around. To avert anxiety, he breathed as Bee had taught him and focussed on the waves and the swooping gulls.

"Is he okay?" He heard Bryn ask Nav.

"He's fine, just let him be."

"When's the court case?" Bryn asked after a time.

"Couple of months."

"The bastard'll be shaking in his shoes by now," Bryn said in a satisfied tone.

<>

In a prison shower-room, miles away, Bill started in shock as they surrounded him. "What's going on?" He grabbed for his towel and found it gone.

"How're you doing, sunshine?" asked the tall one with the tattoo of the snarling wolf on his neck and side of his face. There were five of them, all fully dressed, with hard, unsmiling faces.

"Where's my towel? Stop this nonsense." Hands over his genitals, Bill blustered to cover his embarrassment. When they remained silent, he blustered some more. "Now come along boys. Do you know who I am?"

"We know what you are," said one of them to his right.

Bill looked at his scarred face with its broken nose and hostile eyes. "Now, stop this at once, or I'll call a guard and have you all put on report."

"I don't think so, Councillor Fitchett," the tall one said. "They're all having a tea-break."

Bill felt afraid.

"Don't you remember me?" Scar-Face asked.

"Or me?" asked another to his left, "or maybe it's my arse you'd remember, you piece of shite."

A wave of nausea rose as Bill stared at the man. There was something familiar about his young face.

"Ah, here's your towel," the tall one said, stepping forward and flicking it like a whiplash at Bill's hands.

He yelped, raised his hands, and the towel whipped into his genitals, like an electric shock. Grabbed from behind, a hand over his mouth muffling his howls, he was stung again and again. Released at last, he fell to the floor, damp from the shower and his own piss. Then, the kicking began. He curled around himself as far as his stomach would allow and wailed.

When it was over, the tall one leaned close. "Spike says hello." He dropped the bloody towel on Bill's head.

Bill retched until a blood vessel burst in his throat.

When he came to in hospital, bruised and battered with broken ribs, ruptured spleen and ruined genitals, he remembered what the tall one had said. He couldn't believe it of 'Spikey', the boy he'd raised to be like him. The only one he could trust.

A couple of days later, his lawyer visited to nervously tell him that Spike had given himself up, and was confessing all to the police on the promise of a lighter sentence.

An explosion rocketed through Bill's brain, and all went dark.

Chapter Forty-six

It was unexpected and quite overwhelming. The quayside was filled with people waving and calling his name. He was at first astonished, and then embarrassed, when he saw a banner emblazoned in red letters spelling 'WELCOME BACK KYLE'.

"What the hell's going on?" he murmured to Nav.

"It's a celebration." Nav laughed and nudged him towards the pedestrian disembarkation area. "They're celebrating you!"

As the ship docked, the crowd moved away from disembarking cars and closer to the passenger stairway, and Kyle began to make out individual faces. Andrew's height and shock of ginger hair stood out above the others with whom Kyle used to share his meals. Clutching one end of the bedsheet banner, Andrew yelled and waved. At the other, leaping up and down, was Lola's smaller figure. Therapy group members were there too, and slightly to one side, stood an ecstatic Bee, with Jake smiling beside her.

Jake reached him first, grabbing him in a great bear-hug and passing him on to Bee who cuddled him against her soft body. Kyle looked down to the gentle swelling and up to her laughing eyes.

"Due in the spring. How are you?" she asked, patting his arm.

"I'm fine, glad to be back. Got a lot to talk about."

"Good, but give yourself time to settle in first. I've put you and Navin in a visitor's lodge, seeing as you're engaged," Bee said with a smile. "And your bodyguard's next door."

Before he could reply, Kyle was swept into the crowd and raised on to the shoulders of two men, who carried him, laughing and protesting, to a waiting mini-bus.

Three hours later, stuffed with an enormous meal served at Jake's table, he lay back on bed next to Nav.

"It was good of Bee to give us this place," Nav commented.

"Do you think she thinks we're on honeymoon already?"

Nav chuckled. "Could be arranged."

Rain pattered on the window, and Kyle sighed, relaxed and safe. His mobile rang from the bedside table.

"Leave it," Nav murmured.

"Could be important," Kyle said, sitting up and answering it. He listened to the man's voice, acknowledged his words, said goodbye and lay back down.

"That was short and sweet."

"Not so sweet," Kyle said, turning to face him. "Bill's had a stroke, and Spike's given himself up."

"In that order?"

"I don't know."

The room darkened as the rain worsened and Nav twisted around and switched on the bedside light, giving the room a warm, cosy glow. "What will this mean for you?"

"Don't know that either."

Nav frowned. "Who was that?"

"The fiscal's office. They'll contact when there's more news."

"Do you think it'll delay the trial?"

Kyle looked at him and smiled. "And the wedding?"

"Was thinking more about the honeymoon." Nav grinned. "We have memories to make remember."

Kyle stretched luxuriously, and slid closer to him until they were sharing breath. They kissed. "Want to make some now?" he whispered.

Someone knocked on the door.

"Don't answer it," Nav said in frustration.

"We have to. Everyone knows we're here." Sliding off the bed, Kyle waited while Nav quickly tidied himself, then headed for the door.

Outside in the pouring rain, sheltered under two umbrellas, were five happy faces.

"Red, sweetheart." Lola flung herself at him. "We couldn't wait until the morning."

They piled in, soaking despite the umbrellas, and sat on the couch, chairs and the floor.

"Great to see you," Andrew said.

"Make yourself at home," Nav muttered, handing towels around.

"Did we interrupt something?" Ever-shrewd Lola grinned, pulling Kyle down beside her on the couch. "Let me look at you," she said. Her expression changed to concern. "Your poor face, and what did they do to your hand?"

Kyle felt embarrassed and pulled his hand back.

"I read a book once," Craig began.

"All by yourself?" Andrew asked.

Craig ignored him. "It was sci-fi, and the hero was called half-hand."

The silence boomed.

"But he had magical powers," Craig said, blushing and looking at Kyle with a sheepish expression.

"I think I know the one you mean." Kyle smiled, feeling sorry for him. "Did he have leprosy?"

Craig's face lit up, and he nodded with enthusiasm.

"What happened to your hand?" Ayeesha asked in her soft voice.

Tired of having to share the information again, Kyle played it down. "Lost my pinky finger, and the damn thing won't grow again."

"Does it hurt, I mean where it was?" Sal joined in. "Does it feel like it's still there?"

Nav carried through a tray with teapot and mugs. He exchanged a speaking glance with Kyle. "Can we change the subject, folks?" he asked pleasantly.

Tea was distributed amid small-talk and satisfied sighs.

"I'd forgotten what a good tea-maker you are, Nav," Andrew said.

"You need to taste his curry." Kyle laughed.

"Okay, when?"

Nav pretended regret. "No ingredients, sorry."

As the banter continued, Lola spoke quietly to Kyle. "What about your eye? Is it blind?"

"No. I've to see the consultant in a few weeks."

"Does it hurt?"

"Sometimes." Kyle nodded and sipped his tea.

"What happened?"

Kyle became aware of the silence and glanced around at his listeners. People shuffled in embarrassment. "Okay, you nosey lot. My eye was punched a few times, my fingers were broken, and my pinky was cut off." He waited for the various reactions to die down.

Ayeesha's eyes were tear-filled. "Oh, Kyle," was all she could say.

"I'm okay, really. Tell them, Nav."

Nav held his gaze for a moment and raised an eyebrow. "He's as well as can be expected," he said. "I'm just glad we're where he can get help."

Kyle thought about snapping at him, like he once might have, but changed his mind. He'd mellowed towards him. "Yeah, he's right." He shrugged. "I'm still a bit shaky."

Nav rewarded him with one of his wonderful smiles.

"Did we tell you we're getting married?" Nav asked and, still smiling, sat back amid the exclamations of surprise and delight.

<>

The next morning, dressed for the weather, they made their way to the foot of the cliff and stood shoulder-to-shoulder staring at the rocky, heather covered hillside.

"Are you sure about this?" Nav asked. "We don't have to do it."

"I asked you that last time." Kyle smiled. "Yes, I'm sure. Are you?"

Nav pulled a face, then rolled his eyes as Kyle continued to gaze at him. "Okay, let's do it."

They helped each other, slipping and sliding on the damp, rocky ground, with Kyle having to rely on his lover's better eyesight.

Not far from the top and out of breath, Nav halted them. "This is it," he gasped.

Panting, Kyle looked up at the edge of the cliff. His mind was a blank.

"I said I was knackered, and you said I needed to train more, then, I looked up and there he was." He paused, watching Kyle. "Anything?"

Kyle shook his head. "Nothing, don't remember a thing. What happened next?"

Nav's arm slid around his shoulders as if the remembering would make it happen again. "He reached down, grabbed you, and stuck a needle in your neck." His voice trembled. "Before I could do anything, something hit me."

Kyle leaned into the shelter of his body, inhaling the comforting male scent of him. He strained for memories. For a second, a ghostly image seemed to waver above them like a shadow across the sun, then winked out.

"Do you want to go up or down again?" Nav asked.

"Up and face the demons."

Chapter Forty-seven

Bee's therapy room held a sense of déjà vu. She had scribbled Kyle a note saying she wouldn't be long and to make himself comfortable. As he sat in his usual chair beside the small table with its box of tissues and glass of fresh water, memories of previous sessions crowded in, some very unpleasant. It was a nice room, with furniture one could relax into, colourful plants at the window looking out on to her meditation garden and calming shades of pale green and lilac on the walls. She had a new poster which made him smile; a man's face with words scrawled across it: *There's a crack in everything – that's how the light gets in. Leonard Cohen.*

"Glad you're feeling happy," Bee said, bustling into the room with an armful of files and books. "No, stay there." She smiled as he rose to help. With a thud, she piled them on to her desk in the corner. "Sorry I'm late. Jake decided to call a staff meeting at a moment's notice."

"Is everything alright?"

"Yes, fine, not your problem." She sat in her chair, closed her eyes, inhaled and let go her tension in a long sigh. "Ok, Kyle," she said, opening green eyes now bright and focused. "Tell me what's been happening with you. I suggest you start from the present and work backwards."

It was a technique they had used before. A self-imposed store of good memories to hopefully shelter him from the impact of memories so acutely awful and soul-destroying, that he could be caught in their paralysing embrace for days. The positive memories he drew upon were all about the people and animals he now thought of as family; Aaron laughing at one of Stuart's jokes, Dave chopping wood and slurping tea, big tough German Shepherd, Cooper, rolling on his back to have his belly rubbed. Evie and Lola were there too, and best of all, Nav proposing and hugging him like an amorous octopus. So, when he spoke about his torture, it was almost an afterthought.

"Try again," Bee chided.

"It's like a dream now," he explained.

"You're in denial," she said. "You still have the physical evidence." Gone was the maternal warmth he was used to. Her gaze was unflinching. "When you say he cut off your finger, what did he use?"

"Bolt cutters." As Kyle said the words, it was like he slid back in time. Images rushed past in a blur until he was there again; Bill's feral grin as he said, 'then finger number two,' his helplessness, the smell of his own bowels voiding themselves. "Oh, God," he whispered, closing his eyes.

"Breathe," Bee instructed. "Let it come. It's just a memory."

As he stammered through what had happened from waking up in the coffin through the sadistic depravities acted upon him, he was engulfed by a howling rage. He was aware of Bee guiding him to the pile of cushions in the corner of the room and placing the bat in his hand. He lost track of time as he visualised Bill's malevolent face, and screaming obscenities, battered it with all the strength he had. He came to on his knees, exhausted, with a sore wrist and shoulder, and like a light-bulb moment, a truth filtered into his consciousness. "It wasn't my fault," he said in wonderment. "What they made me do, all those years, none of it was my fault." He sobbed in relief.

"No, none of it was your fault," Bee said in validation.

It was the turning point. Over the next few sessions, something changed for Kyle. Rage seemed to dissipate and give way to a deep well of sadness and grief so profound, it swallowed and enfolded him for days. It came in waves, flashback after flashback of shame and humiliation, until finally, no longer able to cope, he curled on his bed and grieved for the abuse to his body and to his soul. For the first time in years, he also cried for his mum.

He was aware of other people around, at times Bee, Lola, Jake and always Nav sitting sentinel by his side.

Gradually, like a parting in the black clouds, he began to see chinks of light, until one day he woke up and realised it was a new day.

Nav was on a chair by the bed, a book lying on his knee. "Ky? Babe?"

Kyle's throat felt raw and sore. "What's happening?" he whispered.

Nav's eyes were filled with tears. "You haven't been well."

"How?"

"Jake said your mind was making order out of chaos."

"What does that mean?"

"God knows. You wouldn't speak to anyone, except him."

"How long?"

"Week and a half, more or less. Jake's been here every day, gave you some medication. He's an actual doctor. I didn't know that, did you?"

Sleepily, Kyle rubbed a hand over his face "He'd have to be, wouldn't he?" He stopped, something was missing.

"I'll get it for you, if you want," Nav said, "but they reckon you don't need it. Can you see?"

With careful fingers, Kyle explored his face where the patch should be. His injured eye was closed, the skin of his scarred eyelid cool to the touch. As usual, it took longer to open than his other eye. "A bit blurry."

Nav's brows were drawn in concern. "You've to try doing without it. Something to do with your eye muscles."

"Who says?"

"That sounds more like my bolshi boyfriend." Nav grinned. "Jake spoke to your eye doctor. Don't you remember anything?"

"Bits and pieces, like a dream."

"Bee and Lola have been doing shifts with me."

"Lola?"

"She's been great. Got you to eat soup."

Confused even more, Kyle yawned loudly and stretched the kinks out of his muscles. He caught a whiff of body odour and screwed up his nose. "I stink."

"You haven't had a shower."

"In a week and a half?" Kyle grimaced.

"I don't care," Nav said, "but there's plenty hot water whenever you're ready." He helped Kyle sit up.

"Haven't I been to the toilet in days either?"

"I took you three times a day," Nav said in a matter-of-fact tone, oblivious to Kyle's reaction.

Chapter Forty-eight

With a satisfied sigh, Lola closed her laptop. Once she had completed the University application form on line, it had taken her a few minutes to raise the courage to send it off, with a silent prayer to anyone who was listening.

She checked the time, and started in shock: ten minutes late for her group already. A quick shower and change of clothes, and she headed downstairs.

As she opened the group room door, it was to the accompaniment of raised voices and laughter. The first person she saw was Kyle, his blushing face a mixture of pleasure and embarrassment. Next to him sat Nav, grinning from ear to ear.

"I'm sorry I'm late," she said, when the noise had quietened.

Malcolm's head turned in her direction. "Lola. Welcome. We missed you," he said in his gentle tone. "We've just been hearing Kyle and Nav's great news."

"Yes, I know. It's wonderful. I've already been looking for a hat." She exchanged a smile with Nav as he slid up to make room for her.

"We're doing it before we leave the island." Nav said, eyes alight.

Before anymore was said, Malcolm suggested the group settle down. He asked if anyone else had news to share.

"Me," said a voice from the corner. "Me, please. It's Stan."

"Carry on, Stan," Malcolm said.

"I'm leaving too. Joining the army."

Amid the murmurs of surprise, Lola looked at the new, clean-cut, Stan who had emerged from Alec's shadow. Gone was the scruffy, drug-induced hypervigilance. Stan sat calmly, hands lightly clasped in his lap. His gaze was steady as he spoke about his plans, and Lola felt an alarming frisson of attraction, quickly squashed.

"And are you looking at the Scots Guards?" Malcolm asked.

"Since 2006, it's all the Royal Regiment of Scotland," Stan replied with a note of apology. "I've been researching."

"Good for you, Stan and our very best wishes," Malcolm said.

"Good luck, Stan," another voice joined in, with several echoes.

Towards the end of the session, Lola shared the news about her university application, and felt surprised and delighted by the positive responses.

"What course are you applying for?" Malcolm enquired.

"I want to do a social work degree, eventually," Lola explained. "But this course is an introduction, to see if I've got what it takes."

"You're bright, caring and resilient," Malcolm said. "All the right qualities. Let me know if I can help in any way."

"Thank you. I'll keep that in mind." Lola took a deep breath, aware of the reaction to her next statement. "I won't be able to claim a bursary, so I'm going to force my father to give me money."

Kyle was first to react, leaning around Nav with a shocked expression. "You can't go near him. He's dangerous."

"I could threaten to expose him."

"You're only one person, Lola," a young woman called Claire said, her expression worried. "He'll have all his cronies to back him up."

"But she's in a powerful position," someone else said.

"Not as powerful as him," Claire replied.

As the arguments continued, Lola listened unmoved. She knew them all anyway, knew what her father was capable of. A well-known actor, he moved in important circles. Like him, many of his friends had a taste for young flesh. "Who's going to believe *you*?" he'd taunted her when she was fifteen. "You're a drug addict. You open your legs for money, anytime."

"And who turned me into that!" she had screamed in despair.

"Try it," he had sneered. "You won't know what's hit you."

But Lola had a plan and nothing anyone could say, including offers of money from Nav and others, could dissuade her.

Chapter Forty-nine

Seated on the sand with the sea-wall behind, Nav's solid bulk by his side and their friends close by, Kyle felt warm and secure. Lola appeared with a blanket around her shoulders and without a by-your-leave, squeezed between them.

"Hey," Kyle complained, reluctantly moving over.

"Sorry, but I'm so cold."

"And now we are too," Nav said. He slid an arm across her shoulders to stay in contact with Kyle.

Whipped by the wind, sparks flew from the bonfire like tiny missiles, causing folk to jump back with cries of shock and delight.

"I'm so excited, I can't wait," Lola said, for the third or fourth time that night.

"We know." Nav said.

"What time is your university interview?" Kyle asked.

"Twelve-thirty. Yours?"

"I've to see the Fiscal at eleven-thirty. It'll be a rush from the station."

Nav gently touched his ear. "It'll be fine. The boat gets in at eight. The train's at eight-thirty, gets into Glasgow at ten. We'll have time for a coffee."

"Trust you to have it all organised," Kyle murmured as fireworks began to light up the sky.

On the other side of Nav, Craig leapt to his feet with a yell, jumping up and down with each crack and splash of glorious colour.

"Grow up," Andrew called, arm around the tall, slim girl whose hair and temperament matched his own.

At Kyle's side, Ayeesha and Sal were cuddled in together. They'd surprised everyone by suddenly announcing one day at breakfast that they were a couple, but today, they were sad because Sal was leaving Ayeesha behind.

"When you get back to the real world, you'll forget all about me." Kyle heard Ayeesha say.

"No I won't, I promise. I'll e mail and text every day and we can phone at night when you're in bed," Sal replied.

"I'm going to miss you."

"Me too, baby."

It felt too intimate, and Kyle turned his head. The fireworks' flashes hurt his injured eye and he dug in his pocket for his dark glasses. Nav nudged his arm.

"Okay?"

Kyle smiled and nodded.

Bryn appeared and crouched before them. "Barbecue's ready. Do you guys want anything?"

"Is this your attempt to keep your job?" Kyle smiled.

"No way, Jose. I can't wait to see my beautiful girlfriend and daughter." Bryn turned to the girls. "Would you ladies like me to bring you something to eat?"

"What about me? I'm a lady too," Lola chipped in. "I'll have whatever the other ladies are having."

By mutual consent, Kyle and Nav got up, ignoring her moans about feeling cold, and joined the queue at the barbecue.

Once served, they moved away from the gathered throng to sit on a sand-dune above the bonfire. A guitar began to play and they ate in silence for a time, watching a small crowd trying to jive to folk-singing.

"Idiots." Kyle chuckled, wiping his mouth with a paper napkin and taking a swig of coke.

"I never thought I'd say this, but I'm going to miss this place."

"Me too." Kyle agreed as Nav placed their plates on the sand, slid closer and wrapped an arm around him. "Are you all packed?"

"Yup. Leaving some of my books and CDs though, in the common room. Maybe some of the new people can use them."

"Good idea. D'you remember when you first arrived? How long ago? I've been here eighteen months, give or take."

"Two years plus for me, although I had that break after you . . . you were—"

"Kidnapped," Kyle finished. "Couldn't have got through all that without you." He turned around. Nav was very close, leaping flames reflected in his huge, dark eyes.

"I don't know what I'd have done if . . . if something had happened to you," Nav said.

"If I'd died you mean? No way. I'm having my time in court." Kyle paused, "and then we're coming back here to make honest men of us both."

They smiled at one another. Nav removed Kyle's glasses and kissed him, ignoring the wolf whistles.

"I got an email from the minister," Nav said, after a few moments. "She's fine about the date and the fact that it's a same-sex marriage."

"Why didn't you tell me?"

"I'm telling you now."

"I'll text Aaron later."

"You'll see him tomorrow."

"Yeah, forgot." Kyle said, laying his head on his lover's shoulder.

Nav kissed his hair. "Bed?"

Chapter Fifty

The title procurator fiscal had always conjured for Kyle a Dickensian-looking man with a beard and thick sideburns. So, when the small plump woman with blonde hair curled artfully around her shoulders, and a huge smile came towards him, he was uncertain.

"Welcome, Kyle, it's good to meet you at last. I'm Bella Goetz, the fiscal."

Kyle stuck out his hand, and she clasped it in a firm grip.

"Come and sit down." She indicated a group of leather armchairs encircling a small table. "Coffee or tea?" she enquired when he complied. "Or something cold, if you'd prefer?"

"Coffee's fine, thanks," Kyle said, feeling out of his depth and wishing Nav had come with him. He'd left him in the café where they'd had breakfast with Lola. She would have her University interview while Nav went off to explore travel plans to India. He watched the fiscal push the cafetiere plunger and pour two cups.

"Milk and sugar?"

"Just milk, thank you, Miss Goetz."

"Bella, please." She placed his cup near him, and when he reached for it, she gently touched his injured hand, apologising when he jerked away. "What a horrible thing he did to you."

Embarrassed, Kyle nodded and said the first thing he could think of. "So, Bill's had a stroke?"

"Yes, a bad one, apparently, which is why I wanted to meet with you." She offered him a plate overflowing with chocolate biscuits.

Wishing she would get on with it, he smiled and took one, juggled with things for a moment and accidentally spilled some coffee down his front.

"Don't worry. That's what tissues are for." She tinkled a laugh, as she handed him some. When there was a knock on the door, he thought she looked quite relieved. "Come in," she called.

Dressed formally for the occasion, Kyle silently swore at himself as he mopped his tie. He glanced up to see the female police inspector he'd met months ago coming towards them. With the memory, his stomach did a flip.

"Glad you could make it, Max. Kyle, you remember DCI Jones?"

"Great to see you again, Kyle." The younger woman smiled and held out her hand. "And looking so well."

Kyle put his cup and saucer down and half-rose to shake her hand, wondering what was going on.

Once she, too, had her coffee, refused a biscuit and settled into a chair opposite him, she nodded to the fiscal, who cleared her throat and turned to him with a serious expression.

"We wanted to speak to you about Bill Fitchett, specifically about his stroke. As I said, it was a very bad stroke and he's not likely to survive."

"You mean he won't be at court?"

"No, he won't be at court," the fiscal agreed. "That means, there won't be a court case involving him, but we wanted you to know how much we appreciate you coming forward."

Kyle waited blankly for a moment, and when she said no more, tried to process her words. "You mean, that's it. He gets off?"

"It isn't a question of his getting off," she said. "He's dying."

As she continued to talk, he felt his face heat up and a sudden rush of tears to his throat. He wanted to yell and scream his anger and indignation, to toss her coffee and biscuits everywhere and run out of the room. The policewoman came to his rescue.

"This must be absolutely awful for you, Kyle," she said quietly. "It's not fair, is it?"

"No, it bloody well isn't," Kyle said, his voice rising. "How come he gets away with everything he did, just because he's ill?"

"It isn't a question of—"

Without taking her eyes from Kyle, the policewoman stopped the other woman with a raised hand.

"Fitchett is a monster and he deserves to suffer like he made you and all the others suffer," she said. "He was badly beaten up in prison, and we can't be sure, but we suspect his attackers may have been his victims. The beating was so severe that he'd probably have been disabled at the very least, and if that had been all, he'd still have faced you in court." She leaned towards him. "But then, Spike walked in to the Rutherglen police station and gave himself up."

"I know that."

"What you probably don't know is, when Fitchett's lawyer told him about Spike, he had the stroke." She looked at him expectantly and leaned back when all he did was shrug.

"So what? It's not enough. Can I visit him in hospital?"

The fiscal stirred. "That wouldn't serve any purpose."

"It would serve *my* purpose."

"He's under guard, Kyle. You wouldn't get near him," the policewoman said, "and he's unconscious."

Kyle had a vision of himself storming past the guard, yanking Bill from his life-support equipment, throwing him on the floor and stamping all over him. It didn't help. "Can I go now?" He knew he was being childish, but couldn't help it.

"Just a couple more things," the fiscal said. "Your compensation money will reflect your recent injuries. I've made sure of that."

Kyle couldn't care less. "Thanks." He stood up.

The policewoman stood with him. "You also need to know that we're having a press conference in," she consulted her watch, "half an hour, when we'll be making Fitchett's situation public. The papers will make a meal of it, of course, and will be hunting around looking for stories. I'm telling you because they might come after you again, like they tried when you were in hospital."

That caught Kyle's attention. "I didn't know that."

"There was no need for you to." She smiled. "Just be careful, and congratulations on your marriage."

"Of course," the Fiscal gushed. "Who's the lucky girl?"

"His name's Navin," he said, then wished he hadn't when her face fell. "Thank you for all your help, both of you." Aware of them watching him as he made a quick exit, he waited until he was downstairs before texting Nav to meet him.

As he headed for the main doors, a security guard stepped in front of him. "Whoa there, you'll never get through that lot unscathed." He pointed through the half-glass door where a sea of bodies interspersed with cameras heaved in an attempt to manoeuvre the best positions.

"Is there another way out?"

"Sure, where are you parked?"

"Taxi."

"No problem. Follow me."

<>

Nav's eyes were clouded with concern as he listened. They were due to meet Lola in a pub near the university, and Kyle waited until they were seated in a booth with drinks before he told him.

"Fuck's sake," Nav swore. "So, he just gets to die in peace."

"For two pins I'd go in there and shake the bastard awake."

"You probably couldn't," said Nav, in the annoying literal way he sometimes had. "Not if he's had a stroke."

"I know that." Kyle held onto his patience. "It's what I'd like to do though, or batter him with a baseball bat with a nail in it, while he lies there, helpless."

Nav's eyes widened, and for a moment Kyle thought he might argue the possibility.

"Violent fantasy, babe." Nav finally said with a grin. "Can I come with you? I'll watch the door."

Kyle laughed in spite of himself.

"What else did the fiscal say?"

"My compensation will reflect the recent injuries." Kyle quoted, then he paused. "I don't think I was very nice to her. I was a bit rude."

"Disappointment can do that," Nav said, ever loyal.

"I wouldn't care about the compensation, except I don't want you paying for everything."

"Not a problem, what's mine is yours." Nav's tone was matter-of-fact. "You're going to be my husband." He reached into a plastic carrier bag and pulled out a handful of colourful brochures. "See, they're all about India."

Kyle chose one, and they began leafing through it, heads together.

A sudden thought occurred to him. "We could bring the wedding forward."

Nav turned, eyes alight. "We could, couldn't we?" His phone dinged a text. "My God, listen to this."

Kyle tore himself away from bird-watching in beautiful Rajasthan to listen.

"I've gone to see my father," Nav read, exchanging a shocked look with Kyle. "If I'm not in the pub by half three, please come and get me. What the hell is she doing? She can't go there alone."

Kyle checked his watch. "It's almost that now. Do you know where he lives?"

"It's on here. We need to go."

Chapter Fifty-one

Lola paid the taxi driver, promising a good tip to make sure he'd wait, and to be on the safe side, she texted where she was to Nav.

From the immaculate drive, with its tidy flower borders, she looked at the house she'd grown up in. Two stories of solid, grey stone, topped by decorative crenellations, it had the look of a Victorian manse. The drawn blinds, in the downstairs front windows, suggested there was no-one at home. Both locked, the garage door and side gate added to the impression, and she sighed with relief. What she had to do needed privacy and stealth. Stomach churning, she circumvented the lock, slid through the gate and on to the narrow path leading to the huge back garden. As if something might reach out and claw her, she sidled past the basement window. The bars were still there, giving her a shuddering flashback of what the slivers of light had once represented to the terrified girl lying on the bed.

She still had a back-door key – the stupid man hadn't changed the lock – and with a deep breath to fortify her resolve, she entered the kitchen and stopped to look and listen. Breakfast remains still lay on the table, the coffee pot still held a slight heat, but there was no noise. Leaving the door wide open for a quick exit, she moved to the room he called his 'man-cave'. Nothing had changed. The same huge desk and chair; the same silver-framed pictures of herself as a little girl smiling cheerfully at the camera, the same animal skulls on the wall next to the naked portrait of her mother. The proud, Ashanti features so perfectly reflected in Lola's own face, right down to the sadness in the dark eyes.

She bit her lip to stop the tears and reached for the hidden button. The picture slid aside, revealing the safe with its security panel which succumbed when she tapped in her own date of birth. Opening her rucksack, she scooped in thousands of notes piled layer upon layer. Hidden behind was the velvet box containing her mother's jewellery. Her hand was on it when she heard the voice.

"Why didn't you tell me you were coming, Princess?"

She spun around, clutching the box to her chest. He hadn't changed. Still handsome, silver-haired and smiling. It was the tender smile that did it. Even though she knew it was insincere and practiced, it still drew her in, filled her with such a yearning.

"Princess," he repeated. "My beautiful girl."

She remembered. Trigger words from when she was so young. A sharp bolt of fear lanced through her. Her heart was hammering. It was so difficult to resist. With a deep inhalation, she clenched her free hand so hard her nails pierced the skin. "Piss off, you bastard."

"Tut, tut," he chided. "Who's been teaching you words like that?" One hand outstretched, he took a step towards her.

"Stay away from me," she screamed. If he touched her, she was lost.

"Calm yourself," he said, his voice now placating. He was so good. 'Could act Sir Ian Mckellen off the stage', someone once said.

But she saw through him now. Saw him for what he was.

"Keep the jewellery. It was always yours, Princess."

"Stop calling me that, you . . . you bastard paedophile. You fucking sex abuser."

His face changed again. Hurt innocence, quickly shifting to concern. "Still delusional, my poor darling. That place hasn't helped you one bit. Time to come home now, I think."

She wanted to wail, to howl her fear and rage, but that would make it too easy for him. Breathing as she'd been taught, she forced herself to calm, pushed the jewellery box into her rucksack and zipped it up.

"Did you hear me, Zoraya?" The voice of command.

The handles felt good, gripped in her hand like a weapon. "I'm not *her* anymore. I'm Lola, my name's Lola, and if you come near me I'll kick you in the balls." She watched his face twist into a sneer as he moved in front of the door.

"Get out of my way, you fucking creep." She swung the bag from side to side. "I'm going to tell everybody what you are, what you did to me and to Mum."

He frowned. "Back on the stuff, are we?"

With a superhuman effort, she swallowed her terrified anger. "Actually, I've been clean for over a year."

"Heard that before."

"No, you're wrong. I haven't been clean that long since I was twelve-years-old and your DJ pal got me hooked so you could pimp me out to your friends."

"Delusions, my sweet. No-one's going to believe *you*."

"Mud sticks, my sweet," she said and echoed his tone. "The papers will love it. The next adored soap actor exposed as a child abuser."

The mask came off. The face she saw in her nightmares hissed, "Get over here you filthy hoor."

Terror-struck, she froze.

He took a step closer, and jerked to a halt when the door-bell rang and her mobile burst into a jaunty sailor shanty.

"Nav," she breathed as someone began hammering on the front door and shouting her name.

Her father ran out of the room and pounded upstairs. Lola flew the other way, back through the kitchen, out the door and round to the front, gasping to a halt before Kyle, Nav and her taxi driver.

"Have a still tae' wait, 'cause you havene' paid me yet," the driver complained.

"I'm sorry," Lola began and burst into tears. She was immediately surrounded by Kyle and Nav, holding her in a joint embrace.

"What did he do?" Kyle snarled, staring through the still-open front door.

Well aware of his capabilities when defending others, Lola tried to placate him. "Nothing. He ran off when he heard your voices. Let's go. Please," she appealed to Nav. "He's dangerous, he has a gun."

With an incoherent yelp, the taxi driver took off down the drive.

"Wait," Nav yelled, hurrying her and Kyle after him.

Looking back at her father's bedroom window, Lola thought she saw a shape move behind the half-opened blinds, then let Nav push her onward.

Chapter Fifty-two

Nav was on his back, mouth wide open, snoring, when Kyle playfully stroked his nose.

"Eh? Whassup? Ky?" He snorted wildly, thrashing about.

"It's okay." Kyle laughed, dodging his flailing hands. "Everything's okay. Go back to sleep." He pulled the duvet around him and kissed his head.

Nav rolled on to his side and with a final snort, recommenced snoring.

Already showered and dressed, Kyle closed the door quietly and headed for the kitchen. He liked Aaron's flat; five bedrooms; good sized lounge and a huge kitchen/diner with French doors leading out to a walled garden. It belonged to a colleague who had gone abroad to work for a couple of years, so he could only rent; but as he'd said to Kyle the night before, it provided the perfect second home-base for Clancy.

The kitchen was surprisingly busy for so early, but the sight which first drew his gaze was the money lying in neat piles in the centre of the table. At the far end, Evie and Lola sat close, heads together like conspirators.

"Lola's hoard," Aaron commented from where he sat at the other end. Beside him, Stuart immediately rose with a grin and grabbed Kyle in a great bear-hug.

"How the hell are you, handsome? Haven't seen you in weeks." His hug lifted Kyle from his feet.

"I'm great, how are you?"

Stu put him down and regarded him fondly. "You look well. How's the eye?"

"Okay." Kyle shrugged. "Never be the same as it was, but the consultant's pleased with it. Says there's no more he can do."

"Bully for him," Stu said in a sarcastic tone. "I'll find you somebody better. Sit down, have coffee. Where's your other half?"

"Still snoring." Kyle smiled as Aaron poured coffee and passed it to him.

"I like your friend," Aaron said, indicating Lola. "She's quite a character. Told us how you and Nav saved her yesterday."

"She's the brave one, or stupid one, depending on how you see it. Taking *him* on alone. Did she tell you, she's finally going to the police about him?"

Aaron and Stu nodded as one. "She's phoned already," Aaron said. "How did you get on with the fiscal?"

In between drinks of coffee and bites of toast, Kyle filled them in.

"Well, if he's genuinely dying," Stu said, raising his shoulders. "You really can't expect him to get to court."

"They could carry him," Kyle argued, "or film him in his hospital bed."

From the doubtful expressions, he realised how unlikely that sounded.

"Oh, alright." He sighed. "I'll just have to accept defeat."

"It's not defeat," Aaron said firmly, while Stu shook his head. "You're anything but defeated. You exposed him for what he is - brought him to justice."

"But, I didn't though," Kyle interrupted in a heated tone. "He isn't going to court. He won't face the justice he deserves."

"A serious kicking, which almost killed him, and a major stroke which will, is some form of justice," Stu commented, forcing Kyle to slow down and review his thinking.

Aaron leaned towards him, hand on his shoulder. "You were responsible for him getting caught. You were responsible for Spike and all the other bastards getting caught too. You gave other victims freedom and the chance to tell their stories."

Somewhat awed by his intensity, Kyle tried to joke. "Well, when you put it like that."

"I do put it like that," Aaron said, squeezing his shoulder. "That's exactly how I put it. You're a hero."

"Och, Aaron," Kyle mumbled, rubbing his nose in embarrassment.

"Did you tell Stuart about the new wedding date?" Aaron asked with a smile.

"What's this?"

"Because I don't have to go to court now, we're going to bring the wedding forward."

"To when?" Stuart asked.

"We've asked the minister to look at her diary – maybe four weeks, and it'll be on the island."

Stu chuckled and leaned back in his chair. "Okay, just let us know." He yawned. "I'm for bed soon. Been up all night." He rose and hugged Kyle again in the passing.

"What's going on here?" Lola said from the other end of the table. "You told me Stuart was just a friend."

"He is a friend," Kyle said. "One of my best friends."

"Heartbreaker, I thought that was me," she said to Evie and turned back to him. "So, please meet *my* new best friend, Evette Marie, who has given me a place to stay when I start Uni."

"I have plenty of room," Evie commented.

"And cheap too." Lola laughed. "Although I'm a rich bird now." She winked at the men. "Sixty thousand in that little lot and my mum's jewellery, which I'll sell because he bought it as an investment and used to make her wear it to show off. She hated it."

"I'll know where to come for a loan." Kyle winked. "Aaron says you've already phoned the police?"

Lola sobered. "Have an interview later. Will you come with me?"

Taken aback, Kyle hesitated. "Of course, but I don't think I'll be much help. You'd be better with Aaron or Dave."

"No way." Lola shook her head. "You've been through it."

"I agree," Aaron said. "Although, I would think it'll be a different kind of investigation."

"Ok," Kyle said, with reluctance.

"Great, we can all go out for a meal later, on me," Lola said. "I'll book. Can you come, Evie?"

"I'm afraid not. I'm doing something with Cameron, but come for lunch tomorrow. I'll show you the room you'll be staying in. You and Nav too, Kyle" She raised an eyebrow towards Aaron.

"No-can-do, sis," Aaron said, "Meeting Sandi and can't tonight either, Lola. I have other plans."

"You may not feel up to going out celebrating," Kyle said, with the wisdom of hindsight. "Why don't we just get in some pizzas and popcorn and pig out at the telly?"

Chapter Fifty-three

It was a café Aaron would never have thought of going to. More for tourists, he would have thought, or middle-aged, well-heeled ladies meeting for lunch or coffee. Within, an appetising smell of coffee and fresh baking made him realise that he hadn't eaten since the breakfast he'd shared with Fraser. The memory made him smile, and he felt relaxed and happy as he looked around the crowded room.

Sandi was seated at the window, gazing out at the busy street below. Never sure of her attitude, he waited and smiled when she looked up.

"Hi, I didn't see you there." She smiled back. Her hair was shorter, framing her face and she wore make-up. "I've ordered coffee for two and those bacon and brie sandwiches you like."

Surprised, he thanked her as he sat opposite.

"I know you're always hungry at the end of a shift."

Before he could reply the waitress arrived to distribute the meal, and Sandi began pouring coffee and fussing with milk and sugar.

"Where's Clancy today?" Aaron asked.

"With my mum on a playdate," she replied with a bright smile.

Aaron accepted his coffee with a nod of thanks. "Playdate? She's only six months." He tried to make it sound jocular, but something flashed in her eyes before she pushed the plate of sandwiches towards him. "I'm out of touch, of course. Who's she having fun with?"

Sandi looked at him. "Are you being sarcastic again?"

"No, I'm just making conversation." Conscious of her gaze, he grabbed a sandwich and began to eat. "Mmm, good." He raised his eyebrows in a smile.

"I'm sorry, Aaron. I'm a bit tense."

When she didn't say any more, he took a mouthful of coffee, swallowed the remains of his sandwich and wiped his mouth with a napkin. "Nothing to be tense about. It's just a friendly meeting to discuss custody and access arrangements, isn't it? That's what you said on the phone."

"Of course it is. D'you want a cake?"

"No thanks," he said, thinking procrastination.

She had an earnest expression as she leaned forward, elbows on the table. "I know you want shared custody, but there is another option which would work even better." She paused. "I'm not the best full-time mother. I get bored." Her laugh was self-deprecating. "I think it's because I've worked in a busy job for so long. You know what it's like," she chattered on before he could get a word in, "and she's such a demanding child, because she's bright."

Confused, Aaron opened his mouth to speak.

"Let me finish, please. It'll just make life so much easier for us all, and Clancy needs her dad."

Aaron found his voice. "What are you saying?"

She leaned back, white-knuckled fingers wrapped around her cup. "Is it so daft? Clancy needs you. You wouldn't have to pay for a flat and . . . and, I need you too," the last few words said in a small voice.

At a loss, Aaron poured coffee into his cup and, playing for time, added milk and took a sip. It was lukewarm and bitter. He caught the eye of a waitress and raised the coffee pot. "I can't believe what I'm hearing," he finally said. "It's a complete turnaround from the last time we met. What's going on, Sandi?"

She was immediately on the defensive, her voice rising. "That's so typical of you. Always looking for hidden agendas." People at other tables were glancing over, and she dropped her head in embarrassment.

Aaron watched her as the waitress cleared the table and left their coffee. He leaned forward, keeping his voice down. "I'm not arguing with you. I'm just unclear what you mean."

She flicked him a look. "Why? I thought you wanted to have more time with Clancy?"

He had a moment of wondering if they were speaking the same language, then noticed how stressed she looked. "Sandi," he said quietly. "What's wrong?"

When she glanced at him, her eyes were wet. She blinked a few times, but tears leaked out. "I . . . I need your help, Aaron."

"Of course, what can I do?"

She took a deep breath, exhaled slowly and spoke in a rush. "I need you to look after Clancy while I go back to work. Not Afghan, of course, that's all over, but I could get a good posting and . . . and, we always got along better when I was working."

The words made no sense. "Are you suggesting," he began carefully, "that we get back together?"

The expression in her eyes was desperate as she nodded in fast, jerky movements.

"But you know we can't live like that anymore."

"Not even for your daughter?" she spat, eyes alight. "You know, I could tell them about your lifestyle, and you wouldn't even get access."

Ignoring the empty threat, Aaron held her gaze until she lowered her eyes. "What's wrong?"

She burst into noisy tears. Immediately, they were the centre of attention, and two waitresses came rushing over.

"Are you alright, dear?" the first one asked, glaring at Aaron as the other one offered Sandi a pile of paper napkins.

"I'm fine, sorry," Sandi mumbled, when she clearly wasn't. She snuffled and hiccupped into crushed napkins.

Aaron made up his mind, pulled a couple of notes from his wallet, threw them on the table and stood up. "Come on, Sandi."

Still the focus of waitress hostility, he helped his wife from her seat and grabbed her jacket and bag before guiding her through the sea of faces to the door.

In the carpeted hallway leading to the outside door, she pointed to the ladies' toilet and headed off. She took so long he was just beginning to think something had happened, when she reappeared with calm face and reapplied makeup.

"I'll take you home," he said.

"No need, I'll get a taxi."

"I'm parked in the multi-story."

Once seated in the car, she was shivering. He turned on the engine. "It'll warm up soon," he said, lifting the tartan rug from the back seat.

"Thank you, you're kind."

"We're friends," he said, wrapping it around her.

"Are we?" She turned in the passenger seat to face him. "Are we, Aaron?"

"Of course we are," he said in surprise, "We've known each other since we were knee-high. We'll always be friends, no matter what."

"You and your damn loyalty." Her tone was acerbic, but her gaze was haunted and fearful.

Aaron switched off the engine. "What's wrong, Sandi? Has something happened?" He had a sudden thought. "Are you ill?"

The sigh came from the soles of her feet as she slid around to face front again. "Some people would say that."

He waited.

"It . . . it's Clancy."

A jerk of panic, visions of Ollie's little, pale face. "What's wrong with her?"

"Nothing, there's nothing wrong with her. It's me." Another pause. "I can't cope with her crying."

Aaron sagged with relief. He almost said, 'is that all?' but noticed she was shivering again. "D'you want the heater on?"

"Stop being so bloody nice," she yelled, rounding on him. "She cries all the time, day and night. Oh, I know she doesn't with you, with anyone else, just me." She collapsed in tears.

The gap between the seats made it awkward, but he managed to get an arm around her. "This is quite common." he began.

"Postpartum depression," her voice was muffled against him. "It's more than that."

"Have you spoken to your GP or Health Visitor?"

She made a sound between a snort and a sigh as she sat upright. "It's not baby blues, Aaron. Please don't treat me like a patient." She lowered her gaze and spoke to the gearstick. "I cannot cope with her. I didn't bond with her the way I did with Ollie. I don't have patience."

Aaron listened with growing alarm.

"She cries for no reason, sometimes I think it's deliberate, to . . . to wind me up. Last night, I almost hit her."

With a great effort, he suppressed his panic. "Have you ever hit her?" In tears again, Sandi shook her head. "Have you ever shaken her?" She took too long to answer, and he grabbed her bowed shoulder. "Sandi, have you shaken her?"

"Once or twice."

"Jesus Christ," he swore.

"She's ok," Sandi said wearily.

"How do you know?" Aaron yelled, "Have you had her checked?"

"No, but I didn't shake her hard . . . " Sandi began to explain.

Aaron started the car and buckled himself in. "Where is she now? With your mum?"

"Yes, but she's okay."

"Put your seatbelt on," Aaron said as he drove out of the carpark.

Chapter Fifty-four

Nav opened the door, eyes and mouth widening in shock when he saw Lola's emotional state. Without hesitation, he reached to help.

"Can you pay the taxi?" Kyle asked, supporting the girl's whole weight as she sobbed against him. "Went out without any money."

"Sure, fire's on in the lounge."

She was like a child as he sat her on the couch, moving this way and that as he removed her coat and boots.

"Hot chocolate?" he asked when Nav returned, hair wet with raindrops. "If there isn't any, see what's there, herbal tea or something, but not coffee."

Once they'd settled her against a pile of cushions, trembling hands clutching a mug of ginger tea, he explained.

"It's just the impact of going through it with the police. It's very different to therapy."

Nav nodded understanding. "Glad you went with her."

"It's hellish going through it with the police. They make you repeat bits and ask more and more questions" Kyle turned back to Lola. "You did really well."

"But you heard what they said." Lola's voice throbbed with anguish. "I've no witnesses. They'll speak to him, he'll deny it, tell them I'm off my head, and they'll believe him. He's so fucking plausible."

Nav knelt on the floor beside the couch, took the spilled mug from her fingers and handed it to Kyle. "That's what *he* said too, that no-one would back him up. D'you you remember, Ky?"

"Yeah, then suddenly, they started coming out of the woodwork." Kyle agreed, taking Lola's hand in his own. "Dave said it was leaked to the papers. He said it was a fishing expedition, and I was raging with them 'cause I thought they'd broken my confidentiality, but witnesses started coming forward, and that might happen with you too."

Lola was holding his hand tightly, like she'd done in the police station. "Do you think so?"

"Sounds even more likely when his identity hits the papers," Nav said with his good-natured smile. "Now let's get these pizzas, I'm starving."

<>

Aaron readily agreed to Lola staying on in his flat while the initial revelations hit social media and the papers. Although expecting it, Kyle still felt shocked at the huge inaccurate expose in the daily red-tops which seemed to vie with one another for more and more salacious details.

Despite various invitations, Lola hardly left the flat, but spent the day obsessively surfing social media and making copious notes. The situation reached crisis when photographs of her as a younger teenager, with descriptions like, *'Drug-addicted girl accuses local celebrity **father** of rape'*, began to appear. "That picture was taken at my sixteenth birthday. It could only have come from him," she said of one and promptly refused to go outside at all. In an effort to ameliorate the situation, Kyle and Nav hatched a plan for one of them to be with her at all times. They tidied the garden and planted bulbs, worked out with her on Aaron's indoor gym equipment, cleaned the house to within an inch of its life and took turns looking after baby Clancy when she visited.

Three weeks after the initial exposition, Nav's predictions came true. Returning from his morning run, Kyle dumped the usual pile of newspapers he'd bought on to the hall table. The banner headline caught his attention, '***SOAP STAR CHARGED WITH CHILD SEXUAL ABUSE***', it screamed.

"Lola!" he yelled. "It's happened."

Chapter Fifty-five

Aaron paced the small room, debating with himself whether to phone anyone else. He had already contacted his solicitor whose advice was to stay calm and phone him later.

"What d'you think they'll do?" Sandi asked for the umpteenth time.

"It'll be alright," her mum said from by her side on the couch.

"But what if they take her away? I couldn't stand it."

Aaron grit his teeth, to stop himself saying something he'd regret.

As soon as 'Ms Barrett', the consultant paediatrician, had heard the word 'shaken', her previous relaxed attitude changed and she'd asked a series of questions about frequency, how it had happened and had there been seizures. Clancy had been taken for tests and after a wait in the family room, two social workers arrived and interviewed first Sandi, then Aaron, then Sandi again. The waiting was excruciating.

"What are they doing?" Sandi was hoarse with crying.

"You know what," Aaron said, flinging himself into the couch opposite her. "A CAT scan."

"What does that mean though?" Sandi's mum asked. She was a small, slight woman with a lisp, who seemed to have an endless supply of paper tissues.

He looked at Sandi who didn't reply. "It's like an x-ray, Betty, but more powerful. They're looking for head injury."

The woman's eyes widened behind her glasses, and Sandi burst into tears again. "It's not your fault, hen," Betty said, trying to console her with more tissues.

Aaron had had enough. "If Clancy has Shaken Baby Syndrome," he said in a hard voice, leaning forward to make the point. "It *is* her fault, but whether my daughter has a head injury or not, *your* daughter will never have unsupervised care of her again. I promise you that."

Betty bridled, a mother protecting her young. "It's your fault," she yelled. "You left her when she needed you."

Although he believed it wasn't a factor in what was happening now, Aaron felt the stirring of guilt. Before anything more was said, the door opened and in trooped two male social workers and Ms Barrett, the female consultant. Aaron immediately jumped to his feet.

"Please, sit down, Mr Douglas," the smaller social worker, who'd introduced himself as Sam, said with a smile. He dragged over two wooden chairs and sat in one. Arms holding a file to her chest, Ms Barrett sat in the other, and Aaron resumed his seat next to the second social worker, an older man with a greyish-blond beard.

"First of all, to put your minds at rest," Ms Barrett began, glancing between Aaron and Sandi. "The scan showed no sign of a subdural haematoma, and there is no outward sign of injury."

Aaron sighed in relief.

"You say Clancy hasn't had seizures."

"She hasn't," Sandi confirmed.

"Which is good, and there appears to be no history of abuse."

"Of course not!" Betty snapped. "They're both nurses."

The young consultant blinked and pulled her chin back as if she'd been slapped, causing the older social worker to stir. "I'm afraid child abuse does happen," he said in a monotone. "With doctors, police officers and even nurses. It's rare, but it happens."

"So, what now?" Aaron asked, on edge.

The man turned to look at him. "We will be writing to the Reporter to the Children's Panel, and there will be a children's hearing within three to four weeks. We regard Clancy as at risk, and there will be a Child Protection Conference before that. In the meantime, she will go into foster care."

"No!" Sandi and Betty screamed as one. "I'll take her, let her stay with me," Betty begged.

The social worker shook his head, face impassive. "No, I'm sorry."

The consultant rose and with a mutter, left the room.

"Where's she going?" Betty yelled.

Sam, the younger social worker, leaned forward. "Her job's finished," he said in a kindly tone. "It's up to Social Services now. You can't look after Clancy, because she needs supervision and protection."

"Protection from who?" Sandi gasped, her face swollen from weeping.

"From us," Aaron said.

Sandi shoved her mum away and held her hands forward as if praying. "But *he* didn't hurt her. I told you it was *me*." Her voice was rising to hysteria. "Why can't she go to her father? Please—"

She began to wail, and without a thought Aaron was beside her, rocking her shaking body against him. On her other side, Betty looked almost as bad.

"Please let me see her," Sandi begged. "Let me say goodbye."

Aaron looked at the bearded social worker, who shook his head.

"You'll be able to visit," Sam said, clearly moved by Sandi's distress. "We'll set up contact times for you, probably every day."

The other social worker cleared his throat. "That's still to be discussed, but you will have regular access to your daughter." With a nod to the younger man, he stood up. "We'll be in touch," he said as they both left the room.

"Buncha' bastards," Betty swore loudly as the door closed. "Bet they've never had kids."

"They're just doing their jobs," Aaron said. "Come on Sandi, let's get you home."

"I don't want to go back to that empty house. Can I stay with you?"

It was the last thing Aaron wanted. "I'm working, you'd be better at your mum's. He looked down into her desperate eyes and was on the point of giving in, when Betty saved him.

She took a hold of her daughter's arm. "Come on, honey," she said decisively. "Aaron'll run us home, and you can take a sleeping pill and cuddle down in your own bed."

After he dropped them off, Aaron sat in the car and took a few minutes to allow his suppressed reactions to filter through. There was grief and anger too, but worst of all, was the horrified helplessness of a parent bereft of his child. A part of him wanted to weep and wail like Sandi, but instead, he phoned first Cameron's mobile and made an appointment to see him in the morning, then Stuart to make sure he'd be home later.

Chapter Fifty-six

Four weeks later, Aaron glanced around the quiet waiting room at the various people seated in the half-circle. He caught the eye of Eileen, the social worker, who smiled in a reassuring way, making him think that he must look as nervous as he felt. He smiled back and nodded to Margie, Clancy's motherly foster carer, seated next to her. He had attended Children's Hearings before in a supportive role to parents, but to be one of those parents was a completely different experience.

The outer door swished open, and he could hear Sandi before he saw her.

"I know, I know," she was saying to her companion, a rake-thin woman carrying a briefcase. "You don't need to keep reminding me."

As they gave their names to the receptionist, another woman appeared to call them into the Hearing, and they all piled in together.

Aaron found himself seated beside the rake-thin woman, who introduced herself as Amelia Hawkins, Sandi's solicitor. On the opposite side of the huge table sat the Panel of two middle-aged men and a younger female chairperson. At the end was the Reporter to the Children's Panel, a heavy-set man with a pink shirt and floral tie. After the introductions, the chairperson began the proceedings by asking the social worker for a report.

Eileen updated everyone by explaining the background to Clancy's reception into care and her progress since. Margie, the foster carer, then elaborated and Aaron was listening with pleasure to how Clancy had gained weight, produced another tooth and was learning to sit up on her own, until Sandi interrupted.

"Is she accusing me of neglecting my baby?" Sandi asked her solicitor in a loud stage-whisper.

The solicitor made no reply.

"Because until I was depressed, everything was fine, wasn't it, Aaron?"

He reluctantly turned around and found himself looking into the solicitor's pale eyes. To his relief, the Reporter answered.

"Please address the panel."

"I'm ill," Sandi pleaded to the room in general. "It wasn't my fault."

"Mrs Douglas," the chairperson said in a firm tone. "This is not a court of law. We are here to consider the welfare of your daughter."

"My client is simply trying to explain the circumstances," the solicitor said, earning her the full force of the chairperson's steely gaze.

"I would remind you, Ms Hawkins, that you have no legal standing in a Children's Hearing. You are here in the capacity of friend only."

Aaron could feel the woman beside him bristle with emotion.

"To be clear that we're all on the same page," the chairperson continued, reading from a document, "at Sheriff Court on the 25th of last month, under Section 67(2) of the Children's Hearing (Scotland) 2011 Act, the following grounds were proven, A – the child is likely to suffer unnecessarily or the child's health and development is likely to be seriously impaired due to a lack of parental care, and B – a Schedule one offence was committed against the child." She paused, her gaze travelling between Sandi and her solicitor. Neither said a word. With a nod of satisfaction, she turned to Aaron. "I'll turn to you first, Mr Douglas. At the last Hearing you advised that you were raising divorce proceedings against your wife. Has this been done?"

"Yes, and as it's undefended, it should be through by the spring, with custody of Clancy awarded to me."

She nodded and looked at the social worker. "Contact arrangements now and in the future?"

"Mr. Douglas has reduced his working hours considerably and now has overnight contact every weekend and all day contact twice weekly in his home. The plan is that we extend overnights from two to three and so on until Clancy is living full-time with him. There are arrangements already in place with Mr Douglas's sister, to care for Clancy when he is working." Eileen glanced at Sandi. "Mrs. Douglas has supervised contact once a week for an hour in the local family centre. We have no plans to increase this, and Mrs Douglas herself hasn't expressed any wish to see her daughter more often."

"Is this correct, Mrs Douglas?" When Sandi simply nodded, she turned to the solicitor for an explanation.

Head raised, the solicitor took her chance. "As I was trying to explain earlier," she said with a hint of sarcasm, "Mrs Douglas has not been well and is receiving treatment from her psychiatrist."

Aaron looked around in surprise. This was news to him.

"She has applied for discharge from the army and plans to move to another country, so contact with her daughter will not be an option."

The chairperson caught Aaron's expression. "You didn't know, Mr Douglas?"

"This is the first time I'm hearing it." Aaron tried to catch Sandi's eye, but her head was lowered.

The chairperson paused for a few moments before glancing at her Panel colleagues with eyebrows raised enquiringly. They both nodded. "Very well, we shall now move to the Panel decision." Once they had each spoken, she summarised in less formal language. "We are happy with the way things are going and with Clancy's progress. We are in agreement with Mr Douglas gaining custody of Clancy, and once that is complete, the Social Work department should request a review hearing to formally discharge Clancy into his care."

When it was over, Aaron caught up with Sandi in the corridor.

"How are you? I didn't know you'd been ill."

With a snort of derision, she made to turn away to where her solicitor was waiting, then turned back with eyes full of tears. "You got what you wanted," she hissed in such a hate-filled tone that Aaron stepped back. Filled with confusion, he watched her walk away, sobbing. Yes, he'd got what he wanted, but it sounded like she had, too, so why the anger?

"She's an unhappy lady," said Eileen, reaching the outer door at the same time. "Are you ready to increase overnights at the weekend?"

Aaron turned with a grin. "Absolutely, can't wait."

The flat was quiet when he got home. Without Lola's relentless noisy music and chattering voice, it had seemed blissfully peaceful. After Kyle and Nav had then moved into one of Dave's vacant rented flats, it had become almost too quiet at times. Stuart was still around, but other than sharing breakfast together after his nightshift, his presence was hardly noticeable, until he staggered up again to prepare for work. Clancy's presence, of course, added another, usually enjoyable, dimension.

Now, the quiet felt good and gave him time to process what had happened at the hearing. Delight at the decision was somewhat marred by Sandi's comment, and he wondered at the news she was leaving the country. Did this mean out of the UK, or simply Scotland? A job, perhaps, or visiting an army buddy? Was she making the right decision? Maybe he should contact her? Then, it dawned on him that he was doing what he'd always done – worrying about her welfare in the teeth of her disinterest and regular hostility – although she described it as his 'control issues'.

He'd made a sandwich and filled the kettle for tea before it occurred to him she wasn't his problem any longer. The relief lasted until he opened the brown envelope Stuart had left propped against the fruit bowl. He unfolded the document within, read it, and read it again. A sudden coldness in his belly, and his heart began to race. The words were becoming blurred.

"G'morning." Stuart's voice came out of nowhere. "My morning, anyway. Is the tea made?" A pause. "What's up? Aaron? Are you ok?"

"It's negative," Aaron said, dazed. He pushed it towards him.

There was silence for a moment, then Stuart said very softly, "Hell, Aro." He put the paper on to the table. "Sit down before you fall down."

Aware that his limbs were shaking, Aaron obeyed him, and sighed in relief when his friend's strong fingers squeezed his tense neck muscles. "Even though I knew it was a possibility, I wasn't expecting it."

"Of course not," Stuart said, moving to the kettle and switching it on again. "When did you decide to do it? I thought you'd changed your mind after Ollie died."

"Cameron suggested it, with the custody case coming up."

"Will it make a difference to the outcome?"

Aaron shook his head as Stuart placed a steaming mug before him. "It's just him dotting the eyes and crossing the tees." He took a sip of the sweet liquid. As it flowed down his throat, it seemed to release something and he almost wept. "No matter what, she's still my little girl."

"Of course she is." Stuart's voice was hoarse with shared emotion.

Chapter Fifty-seven

"Why didn't you buy clip-ons?" Kyle complained as Nav again tried to fix the bow-tie.

"I thought they'd look more sophisticated."

Kyle snorted. "We're getting married in a gym, not Westminster Abbey."

"Stop moaning," Nav said, yanking the tie from around his shirt collar. "If it had been left to you, we'd be going in jeans and tee shirts."

"A lot less trouble than all this. Who cares anyway?"

"I do."

Aaron watched in amusement from where he leaned against a desk at the other end of the cabin living area.

Kyle grabbed at the tie. "Give it here."

When it looked as if it might be torn apart between them, he decided to intervene. "Can I help, children?"

They turned to him. Nav looking relieved, and Kyle mutinous.

"Proper bow ties, Aaron. Have you ever heard the like?" Kyle said.

Handing his tie to Aaron, Nav appealed to him. "It is a proper wedding, isn't it?"

"Of course it is, Nav. Just ignore him. It's pre-wedding nerves." Aaron smoothed the collar down and winked in satisfaction.

"It's not nerves," Kyle denied. "I feel fine. It's just—"

"Hush," Aaron said, turning to him. Kyle's cheeks and tips of his ears were red. "You're both wound up. It's the biggest day of your lives." For a moment he thought Kyle was about to argue, until tears sprang into his eyes. "It happens to everyone," Aaron said in a gentler tone.

"You too?"

"I was a bundle of nerves. Ask Stuart. Could hardly string two words together." Aaron fastened Kyle's top shirt button and slid the tie around his neck.

"I'm glad you're here."

"Where else would I be?" Aaron spoke lightly, but his own emotions were in disarray. Conscious of Kyle watching him, eyes wide and brimming with affection, he kept his gaze fixed on the task in hand.

Part of him wanted to dance with delight, and a massive pride in what Kyle had achieved over the years he had known him. Another part, curled in the shadows of his heart, barely acknowledged, even to himself, raised its head in helpless longing. As if it was yesterday, he remembered the skinny, injured boy with the huge, hurt-filled eyes, spitting angry words to hide his desperation. Had he fallen in love with him then? Eighteen years old, but still an abused child? Or later, hugging his frightened body tightly, before he bravely climbed the gangplank to his future? All Aaron knew, was when he had disembarked the day before, with Clancy in his arms, and spotted Kyle, waiting in the rain on the quayside, his heart had given a spasm of utter joy.

"Where's the wee one?" Kyle interrupted his thoughts.

"She's with Evie, helping to decorate the gym."

Kyle rolled his eyes and laughed. "Did you buy her a pretty dress?"

"Evie did." Aaron stood back from him. "Is there anything else I can help you blushing grooms with?"

"Traditionally, we shouldn't see each other until the ceremony," Nav commented, from where he was pouring fruit juice into glasses.

Kyle went over to him, hugged him and kissed his neck. "Our marriage isn't exactly traditional, but I'll disappear for a while if you want?"

"No way. You stay put." Nav said, turning in his arms to kiss him. The air seemed to crackle between them.

Feeling voyeuristic, Aaron turned away and left the cabin.

Chapter Fifty-eight

The gym was packed, and respectfully silent, as the young men made their vows to one another.

His duty done, Aaron sat in the front row next to Lola, Nav's 'best woman', who was crying softly into a tissue. He had to swallow his own tears as he listened to their heartfelt words.

Nav's, "I will love you, take care of you and keep you safe forever, my darling," was followed by Kyle, in a strong, firm voice, also declaring his love for his, "Beautiful, adorable, man, who strengthens and supports me in all things and who has been there for me from the first time we met."

At the minister's words, "I now declare you married in the sight of God and this congregation," the room erupted into cheers and wolf whistles. Kyle and Nav hugged each other as if they'd never let go, and Aaron had to borrow a handkerchief from Lola to wipe his eyes.

"That was amazing," Lola said. "Never been at a gay wedding before."

"There aren't many like this one." Aaron watched through misty eyes as the married pair were carried shoulder high, out of the gym and into their future.

EPILOGUE

Two weeks later

Seated in a booth where he could keep an eye on the door, Aaron saw Kyle enter the bar, glance around, acknowledge him with a wave and thread his way between people and tables. Dressed in a navy pea-coat with upturned collar, immaculate-looking jeans, and the copper-beacon of his hair blazing in the lights, admiring gazes followed him as he strode towards Aaron.

"You're looking good," Aaron commented as they hugged. "I can't believe you're the same guy I once ran over."

"I'm not." Kyle winked and shrugged out of his jacket to reveal a pale, grey chunky sweater.

Aaron smiled. "Where's your better half?"

"With Lola. Off buying more clothes."

"Who for, this time?"

Kyle rolled his eyes. "Who knows? He's obsessed." He pulled the tab on a waiting can of coke. "I don't know why he thinks we need so many. Temperatures are around thirty-two degrees at this time of year."

Aaron chuckled in amusement. "I get it that you'll be on honeymoon, tiger, but you will need to put your clothes on sometime. Especially if you're going to meet Nav's family."

Kyle grunted and took a sip of coke. "I guess so."

"That's still on the cards, isn't it?"

"I think so." Kyle waved his can at a passing waiter. "Out the freezer please." He turned to Aaron. "You want a refill?" and when Aaron shook his head, "Nav's uncle still hasn't replied. We're beginning to think it's because of me."

"Being gay, you mean?"

Kyle nodded. "I don't think India's very forward-thinking that way."

"Are you sure it's safe enough?" Aaron asked for the umpteenth time, as the waiter arrived with a can misted in cold vapours.

Kyle smiled a thank-you. "Stop worrying," he said to Aaron. Sharia law doesn't rule in India and anyway, we think Nav's relatives are Christian."

"That doesn't really ease my mind."

"We'll stay in touch." Kyle's tone was reassuring.

"You'd better do."

Kyle grinned and shook his head. "How're you doing? Has the court order come through yet?"

"Next couple of weeks according to Cameron, but Clancy's officially in my care through the children's hearing. I've found a great nanny called Ashley, who'll share her care with Evie when I'm working." Aaron smiled as Kyle widened his eyes in surprise. "No conflict yet."

"And Sandi?"

Aaron shrugged. "Left the country, as far as I can make out. Gone to the States." Although he couldn't say he had, 'come to terms' with the devastating news that Clancy wasn't his biological child, he had reached a place of peace with it. In every other way, she was his daughter and he would care for her and protect her all his life.

"Let's hope she stays there," Kyle said and his expression lightened. "Lola got good news. They've enough evidence to prosecute her father and three other men."

"Brilliant, how is she? I haven't seen her since the wedding."

"Ecstatic about the news and enjoying her college course. The other big news is that Bill's dead."

"When?"

"Two nights ago, in his sleep. Good riddance."

"Is that how you really feel?"

Kyle sighed and thought for a moment. "To be honest, I don't know what I feel. When the court case was cancelled, I was desperate to destroy him, but somehow, it doesn't seem to matter anymore."

"You've moved on." Aaron smiled, watching him frown at the table.

"Bee said that at our last session," Kyle finally said, raising his head. "I asked her if I was cured. She said, no-one's ever cured, but you've moved on and understand yourself a lot better."

"And do you?"

Kyle made a wry face. "Maybe." He grinned.

A man fell against the table, slurred an apology, righted himself and fell again, knocking over Aaron's empty glass.

"Watch it, mate." Kyle snapped.

"S–sorry." The man garbled in a blast of alcoholic breath, as he swayed over them.

"Let's go," Aaron said, grabbing his coat.

On the busy street outside the bar, it was beginning to rain.

"Where're you parked?" Kyle asked.

"Car park round the corner. Where're you meeting Nav?"

"Saint Enoch in . . . " Kyle consulted his watch, "half an hour, but if Lola's still with him, they'll be late." He grinned.

Without warning, the sky darkened and big, fat raindrops splashed on to Kyle's upturned face. It came down like a tropical storm, soaking them in seconds.

Aaron grabbed his arm. "This way," he yelled, hauling him along. Reaching the car, he flung the doors open and between laughing gasps, they both piled in.

"That's some storm," Kyle exclaimed, as it battered on the roof. A crash of thunder made them both jump, and somewhere out of sight, a woman screamed.

In the confined space, they both struggled out of their wet coats.

"Throw it in the back," Aaron said, starting the engine. "I'll put the heater on. It'll warm up in no time."

For a few moments they both sat as if mesmerised by the rain lashing on the windscreen. A second crack of thunder, and Kyle jerked so hard he almost hit the ceiling.

"Where's all this coming from?" he complained, rubbing his deformed hand over his wet face, wedding ring glinting.

"Hang on." Aaron rummaged in his damp rucksack to produce a huge box of tissues. "Always be prepared with a baby." He balanced the box between them. "Help yourself."

"How is she? She was a great hit at the wedding feast, rolling over the dance-floor in her frilly dress."

Aaron chuckled. "She's back into leggings and tee shirts. She's not a girly girl."

"You've decided that, have you?"

Aaron watched him run some tissues over his wet, mussed-up hair. Some bits were still sticking up. "Missed a bit," Aaron said with a smile, smoothing them down with his fingers. Safe and dry in the warm car, the rain drumming on the roof, it was as if they were in their own private bubble, cut off from the wet, noisy outside world.

Kyle closed his eyes, lips parting in a soft sigh.

As Aaron gazed at the beautiful, beloved face, trying to impress in his memory, every feature, every scar, his chest ached with the foreknowledge of grief to come. Kyle would always be around in his life, but never more than a friend. The pain was almost more than he could bear. Drawn by an invisible thread, he leaned forward. It would be so easy to go with the moment, a heartbeat to change both their lives.

Kyle's eyes opened. They were so close. There was a moment of shared recognition. Aaron straightened and turned away.

"Rain's easing off," Aaron forced out. "The thunder's not so close." Conscious of Kyle's gaze, he restarted the engine.

"Aaron, I—"

"Check your coat." Aaron interrupted. "Hold it at the heater. It'll soon dry off."

Without a word, Kyle did what he said.

A heavy, awkward silence filled the car, along with the steam from Kyle's coat as it dried. Twice Aaron almost apologised, then swallowed his words in embarrassment and shame. Kyle's head was bowed as he focussed on his coat.

Reaching busy Argyle street, Aaron parked illegally in a bus lane. He spotted Nav, almost immediately, surrounded by bulging shopping bags and looking cold and wet. He knew he should be calling him over, offering them both a lift, but he couldn't wait to get Kyle out of the car. "There he is," he said. "Go put him out of his misery."

Kyle opened the car door and paused.

"No sign of Lola." Aaron tried to smile.

"Aaron, look at me."

In expectation of he knew not what, Aaron obeyed.

Kyle's eyes were glistening with tears. "I didn't thank you for being my best man. The best man I've ever known." He leaned over and gently kissed Aaron on the mouth.

After an age, Aaron opened his eyes, but Kyle was gone, running through the rain towards his husband.

ACKNOWLEDGEMENTS

Heartfelt thanks go to:

Eddie Small of Dundee University, for his mentoring, support and advice.

Alison Rome, friend, fellow writer and bookseller, for her support, advice and keeping me going through the rough times.

My son **Duncan,** the bravest man I've ever known, for his unceasing support and love.

Phil Doig, friend and 'fixer' for his technical assistance and support.

Sheena Macleod, of **Dark Ink Press,** friend and fellow author, for believing in me and teaching me about the reality of publishing.

Heather Osborne, editor and fellow author.

My two writing groups – **Tay Writers,** and **Angus Writer's Circle,** for their invaluable advice and feedback.

And last but not in the least – my special **Beta Readers**;

Fiona Goetz for her friendship, support and enthusiasm (and for donating her name).

Meg McPhail, Viking Shield-maiden and friend, who fought to the very end and is sorting out the men in Valhalla.

Thanks for reading. If you enjoyed this book, please consider leaving an honest review.

DARK INK PRESS